The Hidden Secrets of a Modern Seer

First published by O Books, 2010
O Books is an imprint of John Hunt Publishing Ltd., The Bothy, Deershot Lodge, Park Lane, Ropley,
Hants, SO24 0BE, UK
office1@o-books.net
www.o-books.net

Distribution in:	South Africa
	Stephan Phillips (pty) Ltd
UK and Europe	Email: orders@stephanphillips.com
Orca Book Services	Tel: 27 21 4489839 Telefax: 27 21 4479879
orders@orcabookservices.co.uk	
Tel: 01202 665432 Fax: 01202 666219	Text copyright Cher Chevalier 2008
Int. code (44)	
	Design: Stuart Davies
USA and Canada	
NBN	ISBN: 978 1 84694 307 2
custserv@nbnbooks.com	
Tel: 1 800 462 6420 Fax: 1 800 338 4550	All rights reserved. Except for brief quotations
	in critical articles or reviews, no part of this
Australia and New Zealand	book may be reproduced in any manner without
Brumby Books	prior written permission from the publishers.
sales@brumbybooks.com.au	
Tel: 61 3 9761 5535 Fax: 61 3 9761 7095	The rights of Cher Chevalier as author have
	been asserted in accordance with the
Far East (offices in Singapore, Thailand,	Copyright, Designs and Patents Act 1988.
Hong Kong, Taiwan)	
Pansing Distribution Pte Ltd	
kemal@pansing.com	A CIP catalogue record for this book is available
Tel: 65 6319 9939 Fax: 65 6462 5761	from the British Library.

Printed in Uk by CPI Antony Rowe, Chippenham, Wiltshire

O Books operates a distinctive and ethical publishing philosophy in
all areas of its business, from its global network of authors to
production and worldwide distribution.

The Hidden Secrets of a Modern Seer

Cher Chevalier

BOOKS

Winchester, UK
Washington, USA

CONTENTS

Endorsements

Cher shines with an authentic gift as an inspirational healer.
Sonia Ducie, AIN. Numerologist and Author

Cher Chevalier is a rare find; a down to earth practical woman who happens to inhabit the psychic world. Approaching her subject with a no nonsense approach, and a straight forward uncomplicated attitude, The Hidden Secrets of a Modern Seer is exactly that – a delicious delve into Cher's secret world; a contemporary account of a remarkable unseen life, which although glimpsed by many, remains for most of us, out of sight.
Jason Karl, TV Presenter and Theatrical Producer

Cher Chevalier is a phenomenal psychic, one of the absolute best. Read this book, you will be enlightened and amazed.
Anna Van Praagh, Journalist

I have spoken to Cher a number of times over the past few years, in both good times and bad. She has always proven to be a valued and trustworthy adviser. Her predictions have unfailingly come to pass, and her accurate assessment of the people and situations in one's life are truly startling. Gentle though she is, Cher certainly does not mince her words when it comes to passing on a message that needs to be heard! For this I am forever grateful. Cher has a great gift and great wisdom in it's application. She helped open my eyes to a whole new realm, and indeed a whole new inner life when I needed it most. I remain forever in her debt.
Natasha Beaumont, Actress

Cher represents a far higher order of personhood than I have ever encountered. Her intuition is superior and her demeanour is very professional. It's an honour to know her and I see great things in Cher.
J D Elliott, Author and Photographer

Cher guides me through problems and helps my mind when things get tough. She is so good at what she does, I feel truly thankful to have been introduced to her. I shall speak with her forever.
Natalie Cassidy, Actress

Cher has been my guide through many troubled times. Her honesty, accuracy and spiritual guidance have helped me overcome many problems I have encountered. She has a calming influence on my often chaotic life and has taught me to be strong for myself. Where would I be without her? I'm not sure....But I am wishing her well as always, and I hope her book helps many others.
Nicola Coleman, Make-Up Artist

PREFACE

The journey I am revealing has not been an easy one – or even what I would consider to be a normal one. From the age of four years when I had my first out of body experience during a road accident, my life was plagued with intense fears, anxiety, paranoia and downright confusion. Up until the age of 19 I had no control over what was happening to me. Neither did I have answers to the doubts assailing me. The things I could see and hear, the visions I had and the energies I could feel around myself and others drove me to the brink of exhaustion and even madness. Facing my fears and literally fighting to keep my sanity has culminated in undergoing a range of intense paranormal experiences, grading at times into ennobling and extraordinary spiritual manifestations which I could never have imagined possible.

As I lay bare my hidden secrets I truly hope to convey, not just how much these trials have taught me and how empowered I have become, but also what a privilege I feel it is to be able to communicate and work with spirit. Since the age of 20 up until the present day I have been working as a medium, spiritual adviser and healer. My client base comprises people from varied backgrounds and walks of life irrespective of class, age, race, religion or sexuality. I deal with a broad range of cases involving everything from domestic issues, spiritual and psychic development, dream analysis and interpretation, loved ones in spirit, psychic attack, spirit communication, business issues, personal and family problems, love and relationships, karmic patterns, past life events, life maps; past, present and future, as well as spiritual healing.

I have been fortunate enough to have appeared on many TV shows with some well known and fascinating people including Derek Acorah , Jason Karl, Mia Dolan, Jacky Newcomb and Katie

Price (aka Jordan). I have been invited to conduct psychic investigations around the country for the Mail on Sunday newspaper and have featured in several magazine articles.

It has never ceased to amaze me how closely linked our world and the invisible realms are. The special relationships I have been blessed to have with my phenomenal guides and angelic helpers, my Teacher and The Great One have enabled me through sheer effort, patience, perseverance, determination, asceticism and courage, to be transformed and lifted from darkness to light!

Having triumphed over the trials, after many a fall, I have come to believe that the whole point of living in this dimension is to be able to achieve spiritual realisation through learning to transmute the lower reflection or shadow of our true spirit self. I hope you will enjoy this very honest book.

Love and blessings, Cher x
www.spiritualadviser.co.uk

INTRODUCTION

My hypothesis, inspired by the psychic and spiritual experiences I have had, is that all universal life including the setting of our everyday world, derives its sustaining force from an encompassing non-physical realm of spirit; underpinned by an all-knowing and transcendent principle.

If we presuppose that we are able to express ourselves because of our rootedness in the hidden dimensions of spirit, then it is reasonable to assume our normal sensory faculties, and beyond these, our psychic and spiritual capabilities, could be traced back ultimately to the inner, non-material planes of existence.

Psychic abilities such as thought transference or telepathy, remote viewing; inner visioning and hearing, clairvoyance and clairaudience, may be demonstrated by spiritual mediums. As the limitations of geographical space and historical time span are set aside, the medium is able to reawaken the subtle links bridging our inner spiritual potential with the all-embracing Divine realm of transcendent possibilities.

I believe everyone is endowed with an innate psychic potentiality. Attuning to such a realm of vital energies is achieved by the practitioner using particular techniques of mental training, possibly assisted by living a certain kind of disciplined life that would deserve and invite in Divine beneficence.

Granting that it is spirit that animates all living manifestation, it could be argued that the purpose of our passage through earthly life is to enable us to learn to bring our individual egotistical wills into alignment with the all-embracing will of the Divine, as we use our sensory faculties along with their inner psychic and spiritual counterparts. Allowing the Transcendent will to bring about harmony in our essentially three-fold nature – soul, body, spirit – may seem hard to attain, but some believe that we are incarnating spirits who pass through successive births and re-births and that we may attain at each stage a higher level of moral and spiritual upliftment.

I will aim to demonstrate how my psychic and spiritual abilities were triggered and subsequently flowered from an early age. Some, if not most of the details I am about to reveal may seem somewhat fantastical. Yet all of us may at some point come to experience the ineffable opening up to aspects of reality not easy to describe or explain in ordinary language except perhaps through simile, metaphor and paradox.

After surviving two life threatening accidents, the first when I was nearly killed by a motorbike at four years old, and then when I was hit by a car at the age of nine, my clairsentient faculties began to open.

I started seeing through my inner vision and sensing forces around myself and others. I often felt that I was being watched by other intelligences. I began intuitively to know and understand the hidden side of daily events and the lives of people I met. Visions and premonitions became more frequent. This caused me great anxiety as what was foretold often came to pass. Initially I had no control over what was happening to me.

By my early twenties, I was spotted by a highly gifted medium, Ben Charman, and I joined his spiritual circle for a couple of years to train and develop mediumship. The more serious training to harness deeper spiritual potencies for healing, remote viewing, journeying into, and functioning simultaneously in hidden realms were to begin in my late twenties. The ability to travel into other realms enabled me to establish close relationships with various minds, from our world and from beyond, some of whom have become my guides. Four of these guides work with me as angelic helpers from the spirit world.

Since my teens, I have witnessed psychic and spiritual phenomena, including people materializing and vanishing before my eyes, but the most potent was when a Great Being from the loftier transcendent realms revealed himself to me, offering to guide and teach me. I have come to call this Spiritual Being The Great One. So powerful is he that initially I was often unable to stop myself from shaking in his presence. Prior to the coming of The Great One, I had dated the most amazing men; but after this a life of strict discipline and ordered ethical behaviour was to begin.

The Great One guided me through a prolonged period of spiritual cleansing and renewal, marked by prayer and meditation as well as the enactment of initiatory ritual practice. At times I experienced mystical rapture, a closeness to the Divine, and this was in preparation for the arrival of an earthly Teacher, so advanced that I was unable to detect his identity or powers until I was truly ready to know.

A harder phase ensued, marked by severe tests of endurance involving the practice of celibacy, abstinence from certain foods and alcohol; and being subjected to extraordinary and harrowing psychic duels. On occasions, I have been attacked by demons as well as dragged from my bed by my ankles and swung round in the air by a lower entity. Some of the resulting physical pain has been so intense that I have had to go to hospital and at one point, my skin literally peeled off due to extreme stress.

I have also had to live with the prediction of my mother's death and I have had to watch and wait for her to pass on knowing that nothing would prevent it.

Now, I have been cleansed and transformed into purer 'light'. I have glimpsed The Divine presence and the intoxicating sweetness of the gifts, the rewards and the blessings I have gained having borne these trials, are worth every moment of torment. The new knowledge and spiritual treasures can only lead me to the ultimate goal, which is to realize true Mystical Transcendence.

It seems miraculous to me that I am still alive and sane having come this far. I have wonderful friends and family around me. I love my work.

My unfoldment continues although I am told I must focus on starting a family, as well as continue with my ongoing daily activity of providing spiritual counsel and prognosis primarily by telephone to a cohort of clients and friends.

It is my sincere hope that this book will help and encourage other seekers along the evolutionary pathway.

CHAPTER 1

THE EARLY YEARS – STIRRINGS OF THE GIFTS

I do not have all the answers to the fundamental questions we all ask, concerning the origin and purpose of our journey here on earth and whether life ceases with the dissolution of the material frame in our inevitable death. I have not yet achieved spiritual perfection. The following narrative is merely an account of the truth as I have experienced it.

My mother once told me that before I was born, I had appeared at her bedside as she lay between sleep one night. She recalled with complete clarity that I stood smiling at her; I looked around ten years of age in appearance.

My mother was educated at a convent school but in early adulthood she felt compelled to explore various religions including the Mormon faith, the Hare Krishna movement and Buddhism. She was also drawn to astrology. She was spiritual and intuitive, with a tolerance and compassion for strangers and animals. Although small in stature and beautiful, she had a will of iron and a very fiery temper.

My father had an equally strong belief in God and a philanthropic turn of mind. He was a vegetarian like my mother, and he had a militant passion for human rights; he appeared on television during his brief political career campaigning for the anti-apartheid movement.

He told my mother several months before she became pregnant that I was destined to be born on his birthday. He was correct that this was my due date, but due to complications, I was born two days before, weighing only four and a half pounds, the weight of a premature baby. After I was sent home from

Cher aged 4

intensive care in hospital, my father took me to the edge of the cliffs where we lived overlooking the sea, and performed what he considered to be a spiritual baptism under the stars one night.

By the time I was three years old and their thoughts were turning towards my education, my father wanted me to be home educated to avoid my mind being polluted by the education system. My mother thought this was ludicrous and insisted that I should go to school and be educated in the conventional way. I followed my mother's course after their separation, which was brought about by a clash of views concerning how the commune that my father had set up should be run.

My first life threatening accident happened shortly after my parents' separation, when I was four years old, when I was run over by a motorbike.

I had gone out with my elder sister to buy ice-cream from an ice-cream van which had parked on the opposite side of the road. We purchased our ice-creams and in my hurry to cross the road, I ran back into the road without watching for traffic and was knocked down. Part of the bike got hooked under my collar bone and dragged me down the road, breaking my leg and collarbone and damaging much of my body. The exhaust pipe had pierced and burned the back of my neck and I had bitten through my tongue.

From the moment of impact, I seemed quite literally to jump out of my body and I remember watching the whole scene very clearly from above myself. There was blood everywhere, my body looked crumpled. I could smell the burning rubber of the tyres and I could hear everything, except that it all sounded very far away.

I was kept in a hospital ward for what seemed like an eternity and when I was finally allowed to return home, it was with a miniature zimmer frame to aid me to gain the strength to walk again. Amazingly, apart from a small scar on my leg and a rather clicky collarbone, the only physical evidence remaining from the accident is the scar I still bear on the back of my neck, which leads straight to the streak of white hair I still have from the shock. The event has left me with an intense aversion to hospitals and the sight of blood .

Ever since then, I have throughout my life experienced the odd time when I have been struck with the fear of continuing to live here on earth, to the point where I have felt a sense of panic about being stuck here in this body and on this planet.

Another serious accident occurred when I was seven years old. My beloved elder sister and I were playing quite happily by the edge of the swimming pool, when we decided it would be fun for her to pick me up and throw me in. She managed to lift me up but then she accidentally dropped me as she tried to throw me into the pool, and as I fell my head hit the concrete ledge and I lost consciousness. I recall hearing noises before I came round again and I still have a small patch where the hair doesn't grow, as a scar resulting from the wound.

My second life threatening accident took place on New Year's day when I was nine years of age. My parents were separated and my sisters and I were now living with our mother in Sussex. I was lagging behind my two sisters as we walked to a local aquarium. My sisters crossed the road safely to the other side but as I tried to join them rather sluggishly, I was hit by a car. The impact bounced me off the bonnet, up into the air and I landed on the opposite pavement, stunned, but feeling no pain at all. I had a miraculous escape and after a thorough check up at the hospital, they could find nothing wrong with me, not even a scratch!

After this last incident my awareness and most particularly

my hearing sharpened and I began to be able to sense or 'feel' and 'know' things. I would have moments where for a few seconds I could feel as being part of the things around me including the sky, plants and the animal world, as well as having the notion that I was being watched closely by other intelligences.

I also began having a very strange vision whereby the walls in my bedroom would suddenly assume the shape of the rear of elephants. I would lie in bed at night and try to shut out the vision but the rear of the elephants would just keep closing in on me, until they were so close I was certain they would crush me.

Only recently the significance of this vision became clear and I was shown why it had kept troubling me as a child. I saw clairvoyantly, a young boy lying on the back of a large elephant slowly moving through some tall trees. As I was drawn in closer to the scene, I could see the tough hairs on the elephant's dry and wrinkled skin. I could even smell the animal and as I focused in closer on the boy, at the very moment that I caught his eyes, I realized that the boy was 'me'; perhaps only in his early teens, very slim and dark, riding comfortably and almost casually on the back of the beast.

The elephant began to plod up a little incline and the boy slipped straight off the back of it onto the ground. The earth heaved under the animal's feet and the beast slid back and squashed him ... the elephant squashed 'me'.

I assume this episode cut short the young life of the boy at that point, as the vision ended there and nothing further has been revealed to me about it.

Another side effect regarding my 'feelings' about things and people was that for no apparent reason, I would feel uneasy or even sick around certain people; at times seemed to have little restraint or control over these feelings when I was small, so I would just react automatically.

One time my mother was having one of her soirees with friends and there were some people amongst the gathering that I had not met before. I remember entering the lounge and getting a feeling about one of the men in the room and saying out loud to my mother that I did not like him. Everyone tried to laugh it off and my mother told me not to be silly and that I should be a good girl and go and play. She then turned with great embarrassment to the man in question and tried to apologize. The next moment, I picked up a very heavy glass ashtray that was on the table and hurled it at the man's head. Everyone gasped and looked on in horror as he wiped the blood from his face. I ran off in tears, convinced of there being something bad about him.

I have to say that outbursts such as this were rare, although verbal outbursts regarding my feelings about people were frequent and of course deeply embarrassing for my friends and family. As I matured, though, I learned of course that one should not comment on the hidden lives of others, but should be discreet and always heed the voice of intuition.

CHAPTER 2

EARLY TRAINING - THE FLOWERING OF THE GIFTS

By the time I was eighteen, I had met and fallen for my first love, but the relationship was not destined to last. As it neared its end and whilst at his house one day flipping through a magazine, I was powerfully drawn to a psychic advert, out of genuine curiosity emanating from the manifestations of paranormal events that were by now becoming a near-regular occurrence in my daily life. I grabbed for the phone and called the number to have my first psychic reading. I was amazed at the accuracy of a lot of what was said as the lady picked up on my own psychic abilities. She went on to say that I could do what she could do and could easily read people. I was so impressed that I told my mother all about the reading. She told me that she knew of a lady called Mary, who was the wife of a work colleague of hers and who was a trusted medium. I did not even know what the term medium meant at the time. My mother indicated that if I must be drawn to such things then she would prefer that I meet and speak with Mary, a trusted colleague whom she knew of, rather than a stranger.

I think perhaps my mother had been expecting me to take things further in this line but until then, she had been a little hesitant. Now she went ahead and arranged for me to meet Mary.

I went to visit Mary at her home and she explained many things to me. She told me that when she was in her early twenties she had been told that she would meet a young lady fitting my description and help her on the right road to mediumship. Mary was now in her fifties. I saw her many times and even suggested that friends of mine should go to her for readings. Mary taught me the ropes including how to read playing cards as she herself did; and soon my own style began to take shape.

Then one evening Mary suggested that we go to a spiritualist church. We went along and the medium on the platform came to us and gave us some very significant messages. I had not been given messages in this way before at a public congregation and I found the whole atmosphere mesmerizing. After the service, which included opening and closing prayers, Mary and I sat downstairs to have a quick drink. A few minutes later the medium, Ben Charman, who had been on the platform came down stairs and headed straight over to us. He looked at me very intently and then asked to speak with me privately. He had the most powerful air about him and the brightest green eyes I had ever seen. He suggested that I should join his 'circle' and to ring him to confirm within a few days. I spoke with Mary about it and she said I should ask him if she could come along with me, as I was so young. So I called Ben the medium and he agreed that Mary could come too, especially as she was a medium herself. We went along that first evening and became part of Ben's 'circle' for the next two years.

From the outset we came to realise that Ben was a tremendously gifted medium. He had worked on platform since he was nineteen and he was now in his late fifties. In the weekly 'circle' meetings, I learned how to trigger and enter gradations of heightened states of awareness, by focusing the mind through concentration, leading to contemplation or the silent intuitive embrace of the realm of spirit. The meetings were held in Ben's home in a special room designated for prayer and meditation.

I learned how to perform protection techniques when entering or retreating from altered states to aid in the transmuting of lower negative forces. As the months went by my clairvoyance opened with amazing clarity and I received many messages and passed them on to the members of Ben's 'circle'. In fact, I channelled so much information that I had to start taking notes as it was hard to remember it all.

Ben was a very serious medium and silence and meditation were the key part of the training I received in his circle.

I remember distinctly him saying to me once with a steely look in his eyes and in a very serious tone, "By the time you are 35 you will be halfway there". In my arrogance I quickly retorted "Only half way there...?" and before I could finish my sentence he said curtly, "Have you no idea that for most it may take lifetimes".

I felt rebuked as a little child might when being told off and learned ever since not to allow my desire for spiritual knowledge, which is unlimited, ever to run riot.

I once went to a psychic fair with a female friend of mine. While there, we decided to go and sit in on a lecture on numerology. We took our seats at the back and waited for the lecturer to begin. It was all very interesting and seemed similar to astrology which my mother knew a lot about. After presenting a long preamble, the lecturer touched upon the concept of people's day numbers suggesting that by adding the numbers together until you reach a single digit, if for example you were born on 19th day of the month, then you would have a day number of 1 because $1 + 9 = 10$, and $1 + 0 = 1$.

She asked people to put up their hands if they had this day number and said a few words about the character traits of each of the day numbers in turn. She continued up to number 4, and I raised my hand with the other 4s. The lecturer looked at me and said "put your hand down" and just carried on outlining the character traits of number 4s. I was a little put out by this, and thought perhaps she was mistaken and so I raised my hand again. This time, she looked at me and spoke rather curtly in front of everybody. "You are not a number 4, so put your hand down".

I replied that I was and she said "when is your birthday? I said the 22nd which equates to $2 + 2 = 4$ but the lady said, "You are a 22 not a 4 and you are here to prove something to the world". She then went on to explain that in numerology, 11 and 22 are numbers which are not added together in same way of any other combination, such as 13 which should be 1 + 3 = 4.

I was a bit confused as to what had just taken place and even more so about the statement she had made. My friend and I left the lecture hall none the wiser really.

It was during those weekly sessions at Ben's circle that my feet were set firmly on the path to mediumship. However I was later to learn and appreciate firstly, that psychic gifts although rooted in the soul-self or the ego, having a mind of its own, are a mere reflection of the Divine spark, the Divine spirit that lies at the core of the essentially threefold pattern of man – spirit, soul and the physical vehicle.

Consequently for the use of paranormal ability to be safe, this ideally could be tempered with the intuitive grasp of the will of the Divine Transcendent Principle. Secondly, I learned that the sprouting of these gifts would not exempt the recipient from existential vicissitudes, which confront us all as we presumably journey from incarnation to incarnation along the evolutionary pathway towards the spiritual goal of self-realization.

Once, just before I turned 20, I had been travelling in a car with an older male friend and had been chatting away and laughing as he drove. In a split second he pulled out casually to overtake a large van in front of us and I screamed, "No!" and put my arm out across to try and stop him, as he swung the steering wheel back in shock. Suddenly a huge HGV lorry went thundering past us in the opposite direction. I could not see beyond the large van that was in front of us but the moment he tried to pull out and overtake, I was like a woman possessed. This saved our lives without question. The HGV lorry would have smashed into us head on. It took my friend a while to gather his nerves again but he managed to stay calm enough to drive us home. He knew of my 'psychic' side but had not witnessed it firsthand before.

Ultimately Ben's circle allowed me to progress in a safe environment to a point where I became relatively more able to manage my gifts, as well as coming to know and build a relationship with two of my spirit guides, who are functioning principally from the realm beyond, having once lived here on the earth plane.

CHAPTER 3

SPIRIT GUIDES AND ANGELIC HELPERS

I grappled with a lot of issues in my daily life and it took me many years to trust what I was told by my guides and helpers in the invisible realm, because I doubted my own psychic abilities. Fortunately they have always been patient with me. I have four main guides who work with me very closely and other occasional helpers in spirit who appear from time to time. Winn was the first of my guides to make herself known to me, and this was when I was only 19 years old. Guides in spirit are always keen to assist us but they also expect us to show co-operation, as like us, they are also travelling along the evolutionary path and are in need of growth and new learning. Winn's techniques were not always of the softly softly approach and on one occasion when I was in my doubtful state of mind, and I kept asking her for confirmation, she actually said to me "Are you stupid?". She was certainly not at my beck and call and would only make herself visible and audible when necessary unless perhaps I was in a crisis. Even fairly recently, Winn has said that she could not respond to me as she was too busy!

Winn's life on earth was during the First World War, and in her lifetime she smoked heavily and still has a wonderful sense of humour.

Whitey was the second of my guides to show up by the time I was 22. He has not had a life on earth for a very long time and when he last lived here, he was a big man who was very much in tune with mother nature and her laws. He is gentle, magnetic, extremely thorough and accurate. Over the years he has taught me many protection techniques and whenever he gives predictions it is always way ahead of time.

In the early days, I would often wonder why my guides wouldn't forewarn me about certain things, even if I asked them to, but later I came to learn that the synchronicity of events, interlinked with individual and collective karma, is so complex, that to have too much revealed would only lead to further confusion and futility. What I did need to know at any given time was told to me and the rest I had to trust to leave to the powers that be.

My guide 'HL' introduced himself to me in a most dramatic fashion when I was 26 and I was visiting an island for a holiday with a friend. I was sunbathing on the beach, soaking up some rays, just relaxing. It was lovely and tranquil with a number of people dotted about and I had been relaxing for a while when I noticed a man dressed in a fantastic attire walking towards us. He stepped right up beside me and introduced himself as HL. He smiled enigmatically and then he just disappeared! I turned to my friend in a fluster and asked if they had seen where the man had gone, only to be told that they hadn't seen the man at all! I had seen and heard HL as clearly as I can see and hear myself, that day on the beach during our first introduction, and not in a clairvoyant capacity but in full physical manifestation. He is incredibly wise and powerful and he only shows up for very serious and specific reasons.

The fourth of my main guides to reveal herself and assist me is Miya. I had just turned 28. Her intuition and knowledge of herbs, medicines, healing and harmonizing rituals is very extensive.

I have other helpers from the invisible realm as we all do, whether we are aware of it or not and I have often been assisted by a wonderful female spirit helper who was a nun when she was last in this realm.

CHAPTER 4

USING THE GIFTS – TESTS AND TRIALS

Shortly before my twentieth birthday, I moved into a flat on my own and my mother gave me a curious little dream book which had no author, as a moving in gift. I had no idea then just how much I would be using it in the years ahead. One afternoon, whilst out walking, I was drawn to one of the little antique shops nearby, went in to browse and came across an extraordinary pack of letter cards. I felt so drawn to them that I purchased them and very soon began working with them in a way I am not entirely sure how to describe.

Almost from the word go, I felt an affinity with them and was intuitively prompted to just shuffle them in my hands. To my astonishment as I shuffled the cards the letters flew out of the pack to spell 'Winn', my guide's name. I was thrilled and exhilarated, but even so I thought there was a chance it was just coincidence, but as time went past and I practiced with the cards, it became obvious that names, initials, as well as messages, directives, and events, were literally being spelled out to me.

As the months went by, my letter cards and my dream book from my mother proved to be supplying me with information regarding past and future events, and after checking with my guides for confirmation, the predictions would come to pass.

I found after a while that I could just 'use' my dream book by opening its pages at random and whatever words caught my eye on the page would reflect exactly what was happening or was about to happen in the world outside.

I did not tell any living person about this for a long time. I would just wait in anticipation and watch in awe as the predictions manifested in reality. I was not even sure if the dream book and letter cards had power of themselves, but what was evidently clear was that they were spookily accurate.

Since I had been living alone, a lot of phenomena had started taking place in my flat. Lights would flash on and off and things would curiously move or disappear and then turn up again unexpectedly.

I had been celibate for almost 18 months since leaving my first love and even though I had many admirers, I had been told by spirit that I must spend some time alone before meeting my next love. I had not realized that some time would be as long as 18 months; or that I would disregard the warning from spirit and start a new relationship sooner than advised. Divine messengers and guides can only proffer guidance and caution, as they do not relish the repercussions of intervening with our own free will.

I was beginning to feel lonely and frustrated and what happened next could and should have been avoided. I was warned by Winn that a certain man who would be trying to woo me was a 'wolf in sheep's clothing' and that I should avoid him. I had managed to stay celibate so far but my own inner monsters ruled by the lower self got the better of me. I threw caution to the wind and got involved with the man, even though he was a fair bit older than I was, and more importantly he was married with a child. He charmed and wooed and pursued me until I gave in. Big mistake. I knew from the energy surrounding him that there was something dark and even dangerous about him, but I found him irresistibly attractive and very physically appealing. He left his wife and his child within weeks and soon he said he wanted to live with me in my flat. I was hesitant as he had some dark sides to his character and he had already shown signs of negative behaviour, and at times, I had seen a look in his eyes that was almost demonic.

After a while I gave in again, and stupidly allowed him to move in, but in less than a week, I knew I had to get him out. He hadn't attacked me physically yet but verbally and mentally he was extremely abusive. He came back one day to find I had packed his things, and he flipped. He was livid and threatened to kick me in the face with the heel of his boot as I sat frozen to the chair. He dragged me and threw me into the bathroom, locking me in from the outside. He left me in there for hours. I was petrified and couldn't stop crying. When he finally let me out he became violent and started pushing me around again. Suddenly the lights started to flash on and off and the big heavy chandelier hanging from the ceiling in my lounge began to swing. He was so frightened that he bolted out of the front door as fast as he could and as soon as I heard it slam behind him I felt comforted and relieved. The lights stopped flashing, and the chandelier calmed and I was safe.

Had I listened to Winn in the first place, none of this would have happened. I felt ashamed and disgusted with myself by the entire episode.

I have since learned that our guides in spirit will not seek to restrain us from using our Divine gift of free will. This is because they are aware that we can learn from the consequences of our actions, where these proceed from the blind dictates of the ego, unbridled by the knowing voice of intuition in tune with the All Knowing and Universal Intelligence which could well be a prompt from a loving guide.

Around this time I had started to feel increasingly unwell. I was having excruciating pains over much of my body and I lost weight rapidly. The pain in my back and neck would sometimes shoot up into my head becoming so intense that it felt like a hot poker and I had to stay in bed for weeks. Members of my family were taking it in turns to come and comfort me and bring me food, most of which I couldn't stomach. My mother was convinced I had been poisoned and my doctor could find nothing medically wrong with me. No painkillers worked and it would take me ages to just walk from my bed to the toilet which was only in the next room. I went down to six and a half stone in weight and when the pains came I could hardly move. Finally, much to my relief, after a few weeks, the pains subsided and I started to gain a little strength and gradually got back on my feet.

Until my Teacher Ray, was to 'arrive' in my life, I didn't know that this harrowing episode constituted a spiritually or alchemically transforming process whereby, undesirable influences impacting on the individual are transmuted into a healing balm for the soul.

I soon got back into good shape. I focused on my modelling career and made up for lost time in my personal and social life. One night I had gone to the pub with a friend, and a man whom I didn't know personally, caught my eye and came over to the table where my friend and I were sitting. He said a few words then suddenly grabbed hold of my hand and tersely said, "Where do you get your power from?"

I quickly snatched my hand back and tried to laugh it off, wondering how he had picked up on my psychic powers and feeling that if he didn't know of their origin I should not discuss things with him.

The Modelling days

In the years to come, my guides were to teach me how to reconcile my psychic gifts with Divine purpose, so as not to earn negative karma. They told me that healers and mediums who use their gifts without thinking of the welfare of their clients build up future retribution that must be paid off. They taught me that the karma of each individual is in the hands of higher intelligences and that mediums can counsel people as they read and help them interpret the past present and future, but they cannot alter the destiny that is there to be played out. Ultimately, it is the will of the Divine that must rule. Each person has inner monsters that could breed anger, violence, selfishness, deceit, jealousy and egotism and these monsters may be rooted in the karmic seeds that may have been sown in previous lives.

By aligning one's will more and more with the Divine will, what is undesirable becomes alchemically transmuted into its positive beneficent polarity.

A medium can help in the unearthing of hidden negative tendencies and perhaps even assist a willing person as to how to handle these tendencies.

By now I had learned to drive and I had my own car, but for some reason on this particular day, I had to take a bus. As I stood waiting at the bus stop, a filthy old tramp approached me and asked me for a cigarette (I smoked in those days), even though he had a half smoked roll up in his hand. I felt sad for him and so gave him one of my cigarettes which he proceeded to smoke. When the bus pulled up the tramp got on too but did not appear to have enough change to pay the fare, so I gave the few extra pence to the driver and he was allowed on.

There were hardly any passengers on the bus and the tramp sat a few rows behind me. We had been going along for a while and then stopped in some traffic and exactly what happened next puzzled me for years. I saw the tramp walk down the aisle of the bus towards the driver and just vanish in front of my eyes. I looked around and up and down the bus in astonishment and to my bewilderment none of the few passengers seemed to have noticed that the tramp had vanished at all.

It was not until years later when my Teacher Ray arrived in my life, that I would know this little episode with the tramp had been a test to see if I would be generous and assist someone who lacked any form of social recognition.

Masters, Avatars, highly evolved entities and humans now discarnate, have been known to manifest physically and then dematerialize – disappear into thin air.

I have also on an occasion experienced another kind of materialization (known as an apport) and this happened one night when a close friend was staying with me. I had had many vivid and lucid dreams, most of which were prophetic, up until that point, but I had not travelled in this way out of my body before and I found the whole experience beautiful and magical. My friend and I had gone off to sleep and everything seemed calm and normal. But during the night, I found myself outside in the cool air standing at the edge of an ocean with Winn. It was dark but very tranquil and we walked happily together by the shore, before stopping to face the ocean and throw little pebbles into the water, all the while Winn was telling me many things.

It was blissful and this was all I recalled when I woke up the next morning and told my friend about it as we lay in our beds. She said she thought it sounded amazing, as she sat up to get out of her bed.

She then began to get a bit hysterical, shouting "Look, look!" and pointing at the floor. I sat up and looked and there were little pebbles from the side of my bed leading in a line to the door. I was as shocked as she was. There was no way they could have been placed there by any physical person as my front door was still bolted securely from the inside, just as I'd left it the night before.

Since leaving Ben's circle after my two year training period, I had not been as disciplined with my meditation practices. But one afternoon whilst I was reclining in the bath, I felt a very strong prompt to sit up straight and meditate. It lasted for a long while and my mind was so blissfully peaceful that I began my regular practices again. I grew stronger and stronger inwardly as I continued with deep meditation, little knowing at the time just how desperately I would be needing this inner strength and resolve in the very near future.

My guides had told me ahead of time that between the ages of 28 and 32, very significant events would take place in my life.

They had also mentioned that I would outlive my dear ones, but they had not fully elaborated, so I simply assumed they meant I would lose them in the distant future. But sadly by the time I was 28 years old, my grandfather who was both a scientist and a comic, passed over. The following year my father was diagnosed with a terminal illness and on hearing this sad news my Nana (his mother) could not bear the thought of outliving her beloved son and began starving herself. Like myself she rarely weighed more than eight stone so when she stopped eating altogether, it was not long before she was hospitalized for malnourishment and when she then refused fluids she passed over within days.

I did see her astrally after she passed into spirit and she looked very sad and disappointed at the way in which she left the earth plane.

My father fought his illness for many months and was in and out of hospital and hospices. Finally, he succumbed and passed over a few days before my birthday. For about six months prior to his passing, my father became highly mediumistic but he would tell me his experiences in confidence so as not to alarm anyone. He would tell me when Nana had been to visit him, which was frequently, and he also kept telling his dog to get down off of his bed, although the dog had passed on years ago.

It is very common for people near death to have visits from loved ones and even pets in spirit; and it plays a big part in preparing them for leaving the earth realm.

The emotional pain I felt when my father passed away was indescribable. I was grief-stricken to the point of utter desperation.

I got involved with an actor, against my guides' advice, and I also turned to drinking brandy to numb the sadness. I had not meant to be disobedient again or to go against spirit's wishes, but the magnetic pull between the actor and me was powerful and the brief companionship minimized my grief.

Pain and suffering are part of everyone's evolutionary journey

Cher as shown in the Actor's bible - The Spotlight 2000/2001

and even the Masters who have come into incarnation and have taken on a human body can still be touched by the pain of the loss of a loved one, although they are better able to handle it.

There are many realms in the world of spirit and we may not fully link up with a loved one from our soul group for many lifetimes. But it is possible to connect with them through mediumship, spirit visitations and dreams.

Indeed shortly before my father died, I had landed myself a leading role in a play having branched out from modelling into acting. A week before the play began, my father passed away. My morale sunk very low and it became acutely difficult to manage getting through the rehearsals. I was tempted to abandon the project altogether until I had a prompt from my guides that my Dad was proud of what I was involved in and that the play ought to continue.

Then an amazing thing happened on the opening night. I was waiting in the wings at 'curtain up' to go on stage as the leading lady. To my amazement as I looked through the gap opening to the balcony, there in the audience sat my Dad, with a huge smile, grinning like a Cheshire cat, showing off his gorgeous set of perfect teeth. And that was it. In that moment I was filled with the courage to carry on, if nothing else, I did it to please him.

In order to cope with the loss of my father, I went to stay with Sam, a close girl friend of mine for a while, but soon after that I went to live with an eccentric couple Fol and Al, until I stabilized. Fol and Al are creative, hilarious and exceedingly adorable. After a few months, with their help, humour, wonderful cooking and crazy antics, I grew stronger. I got back into the strict discipline of regular meditation which Fol soon began to join me in and from this point on I decided that the only work I would focus on was spiritual. In the past I had been a model on and off over the years and I had also had a few acting roles in theatre and film, but all those aspirations and ambitions were now gone. I had worked as a medium since the early days with Ben's circle but I had not focused on it fully as I would be doing from now on.

Then just as life appeared to be shining a little brighter, I received a phone call one morning from my mother, telling me she had been diagnosed with cancer. I felt as if my world was spiralling out of control. I turned to my guides and pleaded with them to tell me if my mum would die from this illness. The answer was 'Yes'. I was devastated. Then I quizzed my guides as to when? But no answer came. I was in turmoil, I had to have an answer for my sanity's sake. I then tried asking in a different way. They knew I was desperate. I asked if my mother would live to reach her next birthday. The answer was 'No'.

I was affected so deeply this time that my life felt as if it were hanging by a thread. What was I to do? I couldn't tell my mother as she could give up hope and I had not been told by my guides that I was allowed to tell her anyway. All I knew was that she would pass before her next birthday which was in ten months time, and until then I would just have to watch and wait. It was agonizing and I was frantic with grief. Had it not been for Fol and Al at this time, I may have gone over the edge.

The days were ticking past like a time bomb and then spirit started giving me messages about my next love who was to come into my life. A little while later he materialized as the fiery musician they had said he would be. I fell for him very deeply and unexpectedly but I still remained magnetically drawn to the actor even though our energies were poles apart. The timing of the musician coming into my life was perfect, as I would be facing my mother's passing in just a few months. He was to become a rock to me at that time. I needed him then and spirit knew it.

I tried my best to prevent my mother from having conventional medical treatment as I knew it would not save her life and I didn't wish her to suffer anymore than she had to. Fol and I took it upon ourselves to look into the best therapies and products available for my mother and I took her to see two reputable healers to help to ease her pain. On the whole she was still looking and feeling relatively well until pressure came from her doctor and the specialist at the hospital, who both recommended strongly that she should have radiotherapy. I pleaded with her not to and begged her to stick with the painkillers that she was now used to, but in the end, the doctor and the specialist frightened her into having radiotherapy by telling her that she could not survive without it.

It was fast approaching Mother's Day 2003, and my mother's birthday was in two month's time, so I knew she only had a maximum of two months left on earth. I had a very strong prompt to now inform my siblings that our mother would not survive the illness, so that if there were any issues to settle or things to be said, as there so often are between parents and children, then they would have the chance to do this before she passed. Once a loved one has gone on, any sense of guilt may prove unbearable. So I picked my moment carefully and told my two eldest sisters. To my shock and despair, neither of them chose to believe me. They had known this prophetic side of my personality all my life and yet they didn't want to accept my 'messages'.

My mother passed into spirit the following month, just a few weeks before her next birthday. She had been in and out of hospital and in the end she was in such pain that she had been taken to hospital to die.

The day before she passed on, I stood at her bedside in a private room and she looked at me and said "It's my time isn't it, Cher?"

My heart was pounding and the lump in my throat felt so big that it choked my words as I tried to answer "Yes Mum".

She closed her eyes again and sighed deeply and then she said, "How long have you known?"

I blubbered, "Ages".

Very softly she went on, "Why didn't you tell me?"

I sobbed that I was sorry and that I wasn't sure if it was right to tell her, that she may have lost hope and I was scared she could have ended it all before her time. Her face looked relatively peaceful and smooth as she lay there and she then told me her Dad (my grandfather who was now in spirit) had been to see her and had stretched his hands out to her. I knew at that moment that my grandfather would be helping her make the transition and that she would be leaving us all very shortly. She passed over early the next morning. Fortunately, my siblings and I were all with her in her private room the evening before.

I was filled with such anger after her passing that a bereavement counsellor advised me that I should deal with my rage concerning my mother having been pushed into the futile radiotherapy, by confronting the specialist at the hospital. I did so. I stated clearly that patients with terminal illnesses should be treated with dignity and respect and should not be bullied or used as guinea pigs.

I then retreated into a deep state of depression and suffered a near mental collapse. I did not feel the need to eat much if at all, but at least I didn't turn to brandy as I had when my father died. I continued to meditate daily, often with Fol, but at times would just sob uncontrollably. I was still getting messages from my guides that I would be okay, which wasn't helping. They also mentioned that I would soon be moving in with the fiery musician.

Then one day I hit such an emotional low that I began calling out to my mother unceasingly. I was desperate and unable to stop crying, I felt as if I had two large vacuous spaces in me where my parents once were. The begging, calling out and pleading to 'see' my mum, went on and on. I needed to know she had gone over okay and that I could link with her in spirit if I needed to. I was sobbing and calling for her when suddenly she appeared.

I gasped and stopped whimpering as I saw her face come into view. And as she moved closer to me, she said, "Cher, please stop. I am trying to rest".

This experience was enough to boost me. I knew I could see her and link with her and even hear her clearly. I know it was selfish of me, but I was so distraught.

Our parents are our passage to the planet and a significant link in the karmic chain that connects us to the earth. My mother, as most people do, need time and rest as they adjust to the state ensuing after death with the period of adjustment depending upon the level of spiritual attainment.

CHAPTER 5

THE ARRIVAL OF THE GREAT ONE

After my mother's transition, my psychic unfoldment continued apace. I came to know even more about my guides and helpers in spirit and my travels in the non-ordinary realms of existence became frequent. On rare occasions I even had a vision of Jesus, or what sounded clairaudiently to me like 'Yeshua'.

The phone rang one chilly afternoon in November 2003 and I was asked to participate

in a TV show with some famous people in the psychic and spiritual arena. I was excited but also a little nervous as this would be my first experience on live television. Once at the studios, my nerves calmed somewhat. I had the wonderful opportunity to meet and discuss matters concerning the paranormal with Derek Acorah, Mia Dolan and Sharon Neill who are mediums, and Sonia Ducie who is a top numerologist, and Jacky Newcomb who has an interest in angelology. The live show featured live readings, phone-ins and demonstrations and it all went very well indeed.

Life continued as usual. That is until one most memorable day. A Great Spiritual Being I have come to designate as 'The Great One' made himself known to me, for the purpose of instructing me henceforth.

I had been sitting relaxing at home when the first wave of his power impacted me. It felt as if I were being drawn out of myself into a boundless space. Similar to my near death experiences in childhood, I could hear everything very clearly but as though it were far in the distance. Light seemed to envelop my whole being, but my body seemed far far behind me. I felt so small, but unafraid. It was blissful and yet so emotional that I had the sensation of my entire being sobbing. Information was imparted to me by his presence.

Then as suddenly as he had come to me, he was gone. I was instantly back in my body, shaking and crying. For many months after whenever he came to me, I was so profoundly affected by his presence that I would shake uncontrollably and tears would swell in my eyes when I gazed at him. The power and authority emanating from The Great One was unlike anything I had ever experienced or could possibly have imagined. The Great One's impact on my inner unfoldment heightened my spiritual awareness enabling me to journey at will into the invisible planes, triggering enthralling clairvoyant visions.

One of these was a vision of a circle of light whizzing round in front of me. It seemed to draw me inside it and straight ahead of me was a large single eye slowly opening up. My attention was then drawn to a bird and suddenly my whole body seemed to whoosh out and I could feel the air all around me as I moved forward. I was above what appeared to be water, and it was incredibly windy but I felt no cold. Then I heard the Spiritual Being, 'The Great One', say "Come with me" and I was taken hurtling upwards at terrific speed and was suddenly up close to the moon.

He spoke clearly again: "I will show you all the things of which you ask", and then I found myself in a totally different setting, very serene, and walking along arm in arm with a lady.

She was wearing a white dress and I wondered if she might be a nurse. Instantly she read my thoughts, smiled kindly, then looked straight into my eyes and said, "It's me" and I realized it was my helper who had once been a nun when on earth. She shared a private message with me and I was suddenly back in my body.

Another experience was when I heard The Great One's voice saying, "Listen to me as you did in the distant past. I will take you to a new place, just follow my lead, do not jump ahead. The full picture is yet to unfold, the right 'timing' is necessary. Give all your confusion over to me". He went on. "I am your Master and you need no other". He then led me through a place resembling crowded streets and up some steps to a building. Inside, right in the centre was an altar with a large globe sitting on it. He said, "Look in it". As I peered in, I saw what looked to be modern studios with TV cameras. And then I saw myself having make-up applied by an assistant. The Great One then said a few words regarding the work I would do in media and television, revealed some information about my father, and the whole scene changed again.

I was getting into an old fashioned carriage on wheels and was wearing a dark green satin dress and hat to match. I was in another era entirely and I realized in a flash that this was a past life of mine. It then faded and he said, "Be assured, all I say will come to pass".

In another of these visualizations, a huge star appeared in my inner view, then figures came in too, men and women circling around with their hands together. One of them spoke and said, "The Great One escorts you and we are to raise you for this hour from earthly life. Be lifted into bliss". And as I was raised up one of them spoke again, "You are seeing the perfection but with some difficulty. Embrace the light that is eternally you and you will see it all clearly. Live it. Your path ahead is guided as you were told before; until your return. Play out each day with The Great One's words on your lips for others to hear."In another of these incredible experiences with the Divine energy, an angelic looking entity with a beard appeared. He said, "Rest and prepare now. You are ever near us in spirit. Beings from on high come around you with knowledge of the eternal".

Then he disappeared and Miya, one of my guides came dancing dressed in clothes in all the colours of summer.

She said, "Your work is for the Divine". As she left a slim bald monk with smiling eyes came and sat opposite me.

Visions of these Divine encounters continued. One time, a large ball of white light surrounded me and The Great One said to me, "Your communion is all that matters. All else will fade. Prepare now and master your body. I am with you".

(I still had no clue what all this was going to mean and I doubted and questioned a lot.)

In one visualization I saw a thick silvery translucent cord in front of my face. It was going through a triangle of light, and then suddenly I was no longer watching but was whooshed through the triangle on the cord.

The Great One spoke the words, "Be peaceful. I speak now with authority. Hold strong for the winds of change are about to blow again. All the signs are proof of my truth. You have but to ask. I am in your service as you are in mine."On another occasion, azure blue was all I could see. The Great One said, "Shh, the shift is here. I am aiming high with you. It is my will that you stay centred and calm in me. You have many busy years ahead in the work that is ours".

He then showered me from head to foot with water and said, "You are clean enough and ready for the next phase."

A golden hue then appeared and inside it was a prism. I shot forward into the golden hue. I was floating in it when I heard The Great One speak again. "You are a worker for me and Divine will. Be still now and hold tight for the next wave."

Then Whitey, one of my guides, came into view and was whirling me round and round in smoke. He said it was for my protection and a source of strength for the future.

The Great One then spoke again. "See the light and know I am here. Lean back now and stay centred as I raise you." Instantaneously I was on a mountain rising slowly to the top. There was light all around it and in the distance a sea of gold.

Journeys to these realms brought a blissful trust and confidence. Another time, The Great One came forward, took my hand and led me to a small garden. He knelt down and motioned for me to do the same. He observed and gently touched some of the things growing there; he said that although they were all individual, they were all One. We then rested there in the lovely garden together for a while, and he told me to trust him and that my faith was growing stronger. That all I could know at this time was known to me and additionally that promises would be kept and my path was set.

Sometimes I was being taught and prepared for the work I was being called to do in service to the Divine. Once, I saw myself inside a triangle. I could feel and hear The Great One but I could not see him. He said, "Do not tremble," (until I got more used to his vibration my body would literally shake). "Two beings assist you, one male, one female. They are of the highest order. They are leading you as a child out of darkness, into the light. Others will try and follow you. The enemies cannot harm you. Leave all timing to us and let others be who they choose to be, for this is truly destiny. Healing and prophecy will be included in your work."Sometimes I was told the mysterious ways in which The Great One moves. One time The Great One said, "Do not look behind you. Behold the peace of the moment. You know of your eternal life map. A hundred times or more you have been shown. One of the many tasks I give you is to lead others to their own eternal map."

A blue light then shot up high in the air out of the candle in the room. "Anywhere, and in anyone, I can come to you with answers and gifts. On your journey many things will be understood about the Earth and the Heavens. Many preparations are to be made." He continued, "Wait with the wisdom you now have in the knowledge that all is for your good. There will be oaths. Love and timing are sacred; try and handle both. In you lives universal truth which is to be shared. Let the petals of the process unfurl."

The visions were not always entirely comfortable but they always imbued me with strength. Once as I sat breathing deeply in meditation, cross legged on the floor with my back straight, a sword at least four feet high shot down in front of my eyes and stood upright spiked in the floor. As it thudded to the ground, and before I leapt up in fright, The Great One spoke authoritatively. "Hush and be at peace. It is the sword of truth. Love of the sword of truth is strong and not weak. Be strong. You have but to follow the steps set out as I have told you. Prophecy and Divine knowledge are to be with you. You will heal with your thoughts. Many eagerly await your coming into your new life. You will not fail. Remind yourself of your life vows. Have courage and use your gifts to slay evil."

My knowledge of my life vows at this point were zero; and as for slaying evil, I was completely at a loss. But would come to know its full meaning in the coming years.

Sometimes I had images of past lives. In one such, I heard people talking in voices unfamiliar to me and then softly came the words; "Come and join us". As I locked into the vibrations of the voices, I noticed to the right of me five men all dressed like sages or monks. As I gravitated towards them, a pain shot through the right side of my throat, and they said this was in effect to improve my communication skills.

For a while now, I had been able to pick up on people's pain and I would often be given a quick sharp pain in my body when reading for people to enable me to easily discern where a problem area was. The five men went on to say that all my fears must be dispelled for me to fulfil my destiny, and yet again, I was told to stop questioning my faith and to recognize my fate; that what I was sent to do was to free others from the darkness of their own mental making.

All five of the sages then added, "Light is all there truly is in reality. All else is illusory". They tried to impress upon me that my destiny must take precedence and that I should pray.

As I wavered in my doubts, my guides were always to hand. Once I found myself inside a translucent pyramid shaped object and my focus was drawn to a fountain in the distance. I was suddenly then up close to it, and could see on closer inspection that what I thought to be a fountain of water was actually a transparent and bright collection of tiny droplets of light. I was bewildered as I stared at the beautiful scene and noticed a little flame inside it. I then realized that all four of my main Guides were watching me study the fountain.

The Guidance was sometimes almost an initiation. Once I found myself inside a white prism and was aware of a very loud heartbeat and had the sensation of being lifted out of my body; and ascending upwards in my cross legged position. A very loud voice then echoed all around and said, "Look at me", and instantly a huge face came into view. I was absolutely tiny in comparison to this male face in front of me and not even the size of one of his eyes.

He opened a large book and after a while looked up from it at me as if in serious contemplation and then to my astonishment, he laughed at me! Still laughing, he spoke to me again and said, "Yes little one, your life is to be in communion".

Then in a much more serious tone he added, "Your guides will assist you with your road to Mastery. Do not push yourself. Choose wisely with your higher self. All is as it should be."

I understood communion to imply the Holy Communion that is given in the Roman Catholic Church but I was non-denominational in my beliefs. I was later to learn after meeting my Teacher Ray, that I was being asked to dedicate my entire life in communion to the will of the Divine.

CHAPTER 6

MEETING AN EARTHLY TEACHER

I had begun to see spirit lights, only the size of a pin head but very bright. I would see them momentarily around people, usually bright white or a beautiful blue. As time went on, I would also see them around places or buildings and often in front of my view when reading for people.

My Teacher Ray

One evening, I was having dinner with an old friend and as we were sitting talking, his gaze suddenly shifted to the top of my head and he said, "What on earth was that blue light?"

I was a little shocked at his outburst and said, "What blue light?" "I just saw a blue light over your head," he said. "What was it? What's going on?"

I think he was actually a bit scared so I smiled calmly and told him not to worry and revealed to him that it was there for my protection. He carried on eating but seemed uneasy as he had known me for years but had never seen anything around me before.

My faith in what was happening to me was tested almost constantly and I was told that much of what was revealed to me was to be kept secret. Embarrassingly I had still not as yet managed to respond to spirit in an instant, or to always fully understand the meaning of a message when I received it. One morning I was leaving the house and before I had reached my car in the driveway, I heard: "Wardrobe".

I thought it was odd and just proceeded to get in my car and within seconds the voice sounded again, "Wardrobe" but this time it was louder. I really wasn't sure what this could be about and as I drove out onto the road the voice came very clearly and audibly loud as if breaking the sound barrier, and the sentence shouted was, "He's in the wardrobe".

I slammed on my brakes, turned the car around back to the house, ran in, and there in the wardrobe was one of my beloved little pets. He must have sneaked in without my noticing. I was so grateful for the message, as I would have been out all day and he may have suffocated in there.

Shortly before my birthday, I was prompted to leave the fiery musician. This was not easy for me as he had supported me so much in my time of need, but deep down I knew I had to move into a new phase of my life. Before this took place my Teacher Ray arrived in my life, but I was totally unaware of his identity and power and the significance he would have in my life as he came to me as a client in disguise. They say that when the student is ready the Teacher will arrive. My Teacher's grace and humility is beyond description and he is so highly gifted that he managed to conceal his identity from me for at least a year. I was literally not able to discover anything more about him than he wished me to know.

Even The Great One and my guides were not letting on. I was not yet ready, nor did I have the humility to be obedient or to accept instruction from any person on earth. Yet this gracious man would be planting spiritual seeds in my psyche that were destined to soon take root. I must say though that from very early on, his voice and inimitable laugh would often reverberate through my mind time and again days after we had spoken when I had read for him.

I was now on the verge of moving into a new property and felt ready to sever my ties with the musician completely. I took the plunge but within weeks I became so distraught that I lost my appetite and began to sink very low. So low in fact that for the first time since my mother's passing, I felt that I couldn't carry on working as a spiritual adviser and medium. My guides tried to step in at this point to give me a lot of encouragement about the future. They assured me that I must go through this phase and face the trials which were part of my life map, and that I could not avoid the tests if I was to move up spiritually. My mother even appeared to me in a vision to show me a glimpse of my future, but even this was not enough to lift me.

I felt alone and couldn't make sense of why my beloved relatives had passed on so young and left me behind in this turbulent world. Why would The Great One and my guides want to leave me to struggle alone without a suitable companion?

I spent a couple of days in bed crying incessantly and sleeping most of the time, until The Great One's voice resounded in a loud clear authoritative tone, as he stood at my bedside, "On your feet Counsellor".

He was not going to allow me to wallow in self pity for a moment longer, or to shirk my duties. "Has all your training been in vain? Be strengthened," he ordered.

Within no time, I was back working and in October 2004 I received a telephone call asking me to take part in an episode of the ITV1 series 'When Jordan Met Peter'.

I was the Medium for the show and was asked to psychically investigate their private residence whilst Katie Price and Peter Andre were present. On this occasion, as with many in the past, I had used remote viewing to tune in to the property the previous night to see what I could pick up.

I had also started to meditate regularly with Ed, an older gentleman I considered holy, whom I had met through my work, and I found this helped tremendously. Who we choose to meditate with is very important. Just as we shouldn't just jump into bed with whoever we meet, we shouldn't just meditate with anyone. It can be harmful, most especially if some others in the group we are meditating with are not entirely sure of their overall motive and intention.

I gained in strength as I kept working and the days went by, but a part of me which had to let go of the musician would not loosen its grip. So I pleaded with spirit to allow me to join up with him again. I didn't believe I was strong enough to face my tests and trials alone. I had kept hearing the word "Reconciliation" which I misread to mean that I should reconcile with him.

As I pleaded with the powers that be one night, a spirit manifested in physical form in my lounge. It had light all around it and although its vibration felt familiar, I could not recognize it. It looked at me with great sadness and disappointment, nodded to me and then disappeared.

I knew quite well that my wish had been granted. Within days the musician and I were back together but after only a few months it was all over. I had made a grave mistake.

I plummeted into a prolonged state of depression and confusion and what in mystical writings is usually referred to as the 'Dark Night of The Soul'.

During this period, I had started to have conversations with the youthful man I would come to know as my Teacher Ray, more as a friend than as a client. His identity would not be revealed for some time yet but I had started to realize that he was the only person I could speak to about my paranormal experiences.

I also consulted with my grandmother (my late mother's mother) about a few of my visions and other psychic manifestations that I was allowed to reveal,as she is highly intuitive and could offer helpful suggestions. On one such occasion she revealed to me that her paternal uncle Robert could levitate, and that the rest of the family considered him odd and selfish, as he refused to consummate his marriage with his wife who desperately wanted children, in case he lost his ability to levitate.

At the appointed time The Great One revealed to me that the youthful man Ray I had been giving readings for, was in fact my earthly Teacher without whom I could make no further spiritual progress. They explained that he had been instructed of the role he would play in my life, as well as where to find me, five years prior to our meeting.

The first time I had gone to meet Ray face to face at a public venue, I made sure that I was on time and I eagerly awaited his arrival. Time kept ticking away and there did not seem to be anyone of his description at our agreed meeting point. I thought it a little odd and so tried to call him from my mobile phone but when I dialled his number, it simply wouldn't ring. It just went blank. I wondered if my phone was okay and tried dialling some other numbers which all rang perfectly. I looked at my watch as the minutes ticked by for more than an hour and in the end I started to feel very frustrated. For a brief moment it popped into my mind that something may have happened to him en route but inwardly, I knew that was not the case. As it approached almost an hour and a half past our arranged meeting time, coupled with the fact that I could not reach him by phone no matter how many times I tried to ring his number, I felt quite cross and agitated and thought of going home. No sooner had I thought this than he rang. Not only was he at the venue but he had also been waiting since the agreed time. It seemed impossible. How could we not have seen each other and why had I not been able to ring him? Then he instantly appeared right in front of me with both of us still talking to each other on our mobiles.

He was smiling and said, "Don't worry, things have to happen when they are meant to and now is the time we are supposed to meet." I was dumbfounded as he literally appeared out of nowhere right in front of me. But he was so calm and seemed so unruffled that I could scarcely believe it. I explained to him that I could not even ring him and tried to get some answers from him but he just laughed and said, "Don't worry." I could only assume it was a test of my very limited patience.

From this time on my faculties began to open up at a terrific rate and I was to experience for the first time what I can best describe as a psychic attack. I had never as yet experienced anything of the kind in all the years I had operated as a medium. If anyone had tried to describe to me in words what I was about to encounter, I would have thought it to be their imagination. I was aware of course that there were lower entities and lower realms and had even at times sensed lower vibrations and seen unfriendly spirit entities but nothing had prepared me for what was coming.

The Great One and my guides had all assured me that I would be safe during my tests and also that I would not fail.

In fact HL had appeared to me and showed a massive gulf between us and had shouted, "I will see you when you get to the other side".

My physical surroundings disappeared from view, then I found myself in what looked to me to be a very dark wood. It was misty and so I couldn't see very clearly. As I walked along I could feel a very negative presence and could also see ahead of me a little rock just a few feet away. I hopped onto it to get off the ground which I felt was unsafe and wanted to check if I could see any more clearly from standing on it to search for a way out of the wood. As soon as I stood up fully to look around, a large demonic entity grabbed me and threw me to the ground. I was shocked and a little scared as it hurt when I fell, which surprised me. I always thought I couldn't be hurt by spirits as I had protection around me. Before I had chance to think any further, the demonic entity jumped on top of me and was so heavy that it flattened me to the ground and started to rip at my skin. I began screaming and tried to push it off of me but the weight and strength of the entity was too much to withstand. As it tore at my flesh I was in agony but with the little strength I could muster, I tried to push my fingers into its eyes and force its face away from me but it just lashed out at me even more. I felt my strength go and I stopped trying to fight it. It lashed at me once more before pushing my body aside with great force. It then stared at me menacingly before leaving as I lay there sobbing.

When I emerged from the encounter, I became hysterical. My face was wet with tears and my body drenched with sweat. I was terrified and turned to the only person I could tell, Ray. I was crying so much that I could hardly speak.

He managed to calm me and gently advised me that I had been in a psychic attack and that when a seeker is being prepared for initiation, she is tested in various ways. He suggested a root of a sacred tree that I should have in the house and to slip a piece of it under my pillow. He posted some lumps of the root to me and on the parcel's arrival I did as he had instructed.

It started to occur to me that he knew an awful lot more than I did.

Before I could move up any further, I was again to be tested. One morning, I woke up to a loud and unfamiliar voice sound "Nemesis". I got on with breakfast as usual and then went for a shower.

As I stood with the water running over me, a female entity came up very close to my body. The power emanating from her and the fact that she had shown up as I was in the shower, rendered me speechless. She offered to grant me powers she could or would use if I so wished. Taken aback and nervous, I refused but thanked her and said I would leave things up to God. She disappeared and I fell to my knees in the shower and prayed for help. What was happening to me? I wondered if I was losing my mind, or if I had gone so far into the inner realms that I was no longer in control of my wits.

Ray told me soon after this event that these entities are also keen to progress along the spiritual path and are able to further their growth by assisting human individuals in our earthly realm, just as we achieve spiritual uplift by living to benefit mankind through sharing our gifts.

May 2005 ushered in another occasion when I was asked to conduct a series of psychic investigations, this time on a range of historic buildings. The handsome Jason Karl was also present, and journalist Anna Van Praagh who was overseeing the project and was to write a feature article for the Mail on Sunday newspaper.

We travelled around to investigate some of the most notorious haunted sites in the UK including Dover Castle, which sticks in my mind most prominently. I picked up a lot of information regarding the locations but Dover Castle was quite something.

I had gone investigating the castle and making comments as I went but after some time I felt that I had seen enough. But just before the team and I had left the building I felt a desperate tug to go and sense the atmosphere in an as yet undiscovered room. The castle guide seemed nervous but readily admitted that yes there was a secret room which I had not been shown. We made our way following her lead. As I trod up the stone steps to the hidden room, my heart began pounding. I felt nauseous and light headed. The rest of the team stayed and watched from the bottom of the stone steps as I reached the heavy solid door. It was locked. No access was allowed. Not even to any of us on the investigation. I was relieved in a way. Just being on the outside the little chamber was draining enough. I have rarely felt such negative energy in a place.

I sat on the top stair close to the door and repeated a prayer over and over and over. When I was prompted by spirit to leave shortly after, I felt quite weak. The whole experience had been overwhelming and most surprising.

Once when I was travelling on the train to meet with the older gentleman Ed for meditation, I suddenly saw myself in a scene that was very beautiful and as I looked around I saw Yeshua. He gently took my right hand in his left hand and we started to walk together side by side and I noticed as we walked that flowers were falling all around us. As I realized the magnitude of who he was, I tried to pull my hand back from his as I felt so small and unworthy, but he persisted and said, "Come and walk with me," and as we walked on hand in hand, my feelings of self disgust suddenly diminished.

The scene faded and to get a sense of being back in the physical realm, I shifted my gaze to the other passengers on the train and noticed that just above the seat in front of me, the back of a baby's head popped into view. I could hear the couple sitting in the seats in front talking and I was just enjoying looking at the baby's soft brown hair shining in the sunlight. I felt comforted by the normality of it and leaned up in my seat to see the baby more clearly, but to my surprise only the couple were sat there. I assumed that the baby I had seen was either one they had lost or not yet had.

In another vision, a small white arrow-head went into the top of my skull and The Great One said "Divine Will be instilled in you. Lead others and follow me."

My guide HL was also sitting cross legged on the floor in the middle of the room and he motioned for me to come over to him and I did so but I felt restless and paced up and down close by him. He sat very still and contentedly asking me to sit opposite him on the floor. As I did so, he took both of my hands in his and I instantly felt very calm.

To the right of the room there then appeared to be a little opening I hadn't noticed before. The Great One appeared in it and stood motionless as he communicated things to me telepathically. He then looked over towards a doorway which had just appeared behind HL and said to me, "When you are ready, go through it".

I had been instructed to follow a form of self-denial which included the practice of celibacy, abstinence from certain foods and alcohol and limiting my social engagements. I struggled tremendously with the practice of asceticism and the intense emotional strain I was undergoing, but at times I was able to still my mind through silent prayer and meditation.

Meanwhile my psychic experiences continued to unfurl. My mind got flooded with pictures and memories of my past lives, some of which were hideous. I began to get flashes of past life errors which would be so magnified that even though I pleaded for forgiveness, I continued at times to be swept over by a heavy sense of guilt and shame for days. The smallest details from my past would be shown to me and played out as a scene. Every lie I had ever told, every word I had spoken unkindly and every hurt I had caused anyone. Ray kept telling me not to worry to just keep praying to the Divine.

Then one day The Great One called out: "On your knees!" I did as he had said and as I prayed I started to sob. I do not know how long I was on my knees with my head on the floor but when I got up it was difficult to stand with my legs straight and I had deep marks on my forehead.

After this, Ray sent me a book on mysticism to read, which I found considerably helpful and comforting. I had thought I was losing my mind, but since reading that other students of mysticism had also experienced altered states, as well as occasional flows of excruciating pains shooting through the body, it was clear I was sane and not alone in my experiences. Ray assured me that the pains were the physical manifestations of an inner process of spiritual cleansing. Some of these pains were so intense that I even went to hospital, but of course nothing untoward was found. My Teacher seemed amused that I had been to hospital for a check-up and then went on to say in a serious tone, "If we do not forgive we cannot go to God".

I had been hearing at this time the word "War" clairaudiently and not too long after I heard very clearly, "There is a war going on. You must fight".

I took this to mean that I must face my trials with more

courage. But the message carried a far more potent meaning concerning how my future was to unfold. I then had an inner vision of Ray's Teacher, SEG who lives in another part of the world.

The energy surrounding him was so enthralling that I mistakenly assumed that he was a highly evolved being in spirit and not in a physical body here on earth. I saw him in a seated position but then he suddenly turned himself upside down in the air, still in his seated position! He smiled and said, "It's easy to escape this realm but not essential."

He then asked me to hold out my hand and as he looked closely at my palm a pain shot through my right arm and then my left foot. He stared at me and then said, "Arise" and he was spinning me round with my bare feet on the dusty ground.

He put some wet mud on my left foot and across my right palm and pushed me back into my seat and then moved his thumb across my forehead. I was later to learn that the ritual administered was a type of initiation.

A few nights later I experienced being rolled up in a ball at The Great One's feet. Although he always radiated a tremendous amount of energy and light, I could now be in his presence without feeling tearful and shaking as had happened before. I was told that lower entities do not have any influence over The Great One and that he laughs at them, regarding them as naughty children.

Following the experience with The Great One I had been looking out of the window at the view consisting of a few houses, some greenery and the sea. As I was admiring the scene, there appeared to be what I can only describe as a gap in the view. I blinked a few times just to be sure there was nothing on the glass to obscure the view but the gap was still visible in the scene. It was as if I was looking at a lovely picture with a piece of the middle torn out. The scene faded soon after and the view returned in its normal form. A couple of days later, the experience repeated itself. This time there was more than one gap in the view and I could also see other buildings that are not usually there as well as boats on the sea and the sun seemed to be pulsating in the sky.

As I looked on in bemusement I heard, "Be above pain and pleasure, matter keeps transforming for as long as God wills." And once again the view returned to its natural state.

I simply had to call Ray and tell him about the experience. He was as patient and as empowering as ever and also very happy about the multidimensional scene I had witnessed. He said with a little laugh, "A prophetess and a mystic".

The next time I saw The Great One, he had said that I was being watched closely and if I listened carefully I would come to a fuller understanding. I then saw the fountain of light droplets I had witnessed in the past, but this time the light was inside me! After this I was shown a most unusual and spectacular ritual. The Great One appeared to be spinning around with a sword outstretched in his hands and a circle of people some of whom I recognized were lying on the ground. It quickly became obvious to me that the people had been struck down by his sword as he had spun round with it. The Great One then focused on the one person left standing and gently pushed her over with the tip of his sword and she also fell to the ground.

I had never seen him perform in this way before. He still looked very calm but so serious that I did not even dare to ask what he was doing. Then one of the people on the ground raised his head and stretched out his hand for help.

I waited to watch The Great One's reaction and he indicated that the person would have to crawl out of there on his own. Within a very short time, the people I had recognized as being in the circle at the time, had things happening to them, some of which were quite harrowing. These people were apparently paying off their karmic debts.

The Great One and my Teacher Ray continued to educate me

and test me in a myriad of ways to ensure that I could be trusted with the knowledge being revealed. Most of the time, I was advised not to tell anyone of the information being passed on to me and on rare occasions, I was even told not to repeat things to Ray that spirit had told me. I took this as a test of my obedience. In the coming year, I would also be taught how to use my gifts silently and that as I came to handle the contradictions, I would learn that living what you tell others is the best way to teach.

The highs and lows I was going through were at times extreme. It was during one of my lows that The Great One came to me and said, "You make me feel ashamed of you," which made me feel awful and ridiculous. When I had found my balance again he said, "People must be loved, but not trusted fully until they have conquered the lower self , trust has to be earned. I will now be working from the inside."

But I couldn't fathom the meaning of his last statement just yet.

Days drifted into weeks and weeks into months and apart from looking a little tired and even thinner than usual, I appeared the same but the transition was far from over.

At this time, I had another past life experience and saw myself in a velvet fitted bodice and a skirt flowing down to the floor. I could feel how soft the fabric was against my skin. I looked very similar in features to how I do now but my hair was down past my waist in length. I was standing in a stone building looking out onto the dark streets below in the distance.

The Great One had taught me to practice a new protection technique as well as a new way of directing my thought. He had spoken to me about Life Water and had poured some of it over me saying I was a filter that must be cleansed. He said I could plead if I must when in need of help and that I must take up my guard, as it was now time to go forward and to become harmless and stay in harmony.

A few nights later, I had a hideous nightmare in which much

about the human degeneracy was shown to me.

As the days went by I was feeling increasingly in need of safety. The anxiety would come and go in waves as would the tears and feelings of self disgust.

By now, I had heard clairaudiently and had 'psychic post' delivered to reveal that a lot of my eclectic circle of friends were beginning to talk about me. Some of what they said was founded in concern and some of it was gossip, which hurt me somewhat, but I couldn't have tried to explain and enlighten them as to what was happening to me as I had been told plainly to keep things hidden for now.

During this period I saw my Dad one afternoon when I had retired to bed, feeling ill with pains in my body again, and as I lay there trying to stay calm, a very subtle golden mist formed around me.

The Great One then appeared and stood in front of me. He had a demonic entity standing at his side and the two of them just stood facing me. Before I had time to question The Great One, the demon tried to rush forward to attack me. I reeled back in horror but then realized it couldn't invade my energy field; which seemed like an invisible shield. The demon figure seemed stunned and stepped back.

The Great One then spoke and his words were like music to my ears. He said he had made me strong. The pains then subsided and I enjoyed a deep and peaceful sleep.

Less than a week later, HL came before me and in a swift action pointed a sword at my throat. I was frozen with fear as he touched the tip to my skin and then thrust it into my neck. I expected to feel pain but the instrument disappeared into light!

I picked up clairaudiently that my life would soon switch into a new stream. My mother and Winn both showed up standing side by side looking happy and excited as they gave me a clip of what lay ahead in my private life.

CHAPTER 7

EXPANSION OF MY SPIRITUAL AWARENESS

In recent years I have come to experience what may be regarded as mystical illumination; that is, a direct intuitive contact, supremely blissful involving the cessation of all physiological and mental activity, with The Absolute Divine ground of existence.

I now know that a good number of my paranormal experiences of the past, although intense and overpowering, cannot be described as mystical insofar as they contained elements of our normal sensual reality.

It seems to me that what precedes the dawning of a true mystical union is usually a period during which the aspirant is led through a phase of earthly tests and trials, as a way of aiding them to adapt to the new order for soul expression, that the opening up of consciousness and initiatory awakening will be calling for.

At this point it is possible that someone on their spiritual path will have to contend with the problem of moving amongst friends and foe alike, who may mistrust or misconstrue the new mode of life that they will demonstrate hereafter.

Being on the spiritual path will have drawn the ineffable into their expanding consciousness. Language will sometimes fail them in the struggle to communicate in words the inexpressible.

I was prompted one night to go and light a candle and to pray on my knees. Within moments, my heart was pounding and the presence around me was so powerful and sublime, I thought I would faint. I felt about the size of an ant and panted heavily as I breathed. Words seemed to come from everywhere. I couldn't see anything but I heard a ubiquitous voice sound "Honour ME with silence".

I felt so fragile that I could shatter and was seized with awe. Then again more words sounded: "The heart is the power centre of spirit and body".

I was then alone again, the presence had gone. When my breathing became normal again, I felt like crying but instead I jumped for joy once I had regained composure.

During the World Cup in May 2006, I was contacted and asked to conduct absent healing for the talented footballer Wayne Rooney to assist him to recover from an injury so that he could return to the World Cup event. My role was televised on Sky One at the Celebrity World Cup Soccer football stadium. Hilariously, I was mistaken for the model Caprice in the make-up room.

I was given a room to work in privately and once I had blocked out the outside noises, I tuned in, meditated for a while, and to my astonishment The Great One materialized in front of me. I was not sure as to who would be assisting me from the invisible realm on this occasion and was delighted when he showed up.

He was very serious in his tone, and spoke softly as he led me through some focusing exercises and a healing ritual; after which he said with a smile, "The healing can begin".

A few days afterwards, I had a personal message from spirit telling me that I had "Clearance and permission". For what I didn't know yet. I got in the shower and The Great One appeared on my left and asked me if I was ready?

He then showed me a barren wasteland and with a wave of his hand, a city, as he smiled.

I knew intuitively this was regarding my future. For some time I had been shown glimpses of my partner to be, including his hair colour, and had been given hints as to his birth sign and a few other details about his life, but I was not certain exactly who he was as I knew a lot of raven haired bachelors matching his description.

The Great One then came again, knelt before me and took my hands in his. He said that I must be holy and confident and that I now had the power to transmute and alter the flow of thought patterns. He said that all beings, everyone and everything, even demons, must come to the Divine.

The next day, I found myself once again in a state of ecstasy without any conscious awareness of my surroundings, let alone my body. Whilst emerging from this state; the omnipresent voice sounded, "As long as your heart is beating I am with you, when it stops, you will be with Me. This is realization. No power can separate Us." Once alone and feeling delicate, The Great One appeared in a vision. He was in a little boat and motioned for me to get in for a training session. The water appeared still as we rowed out and he asked me to focus on him as he was helping me to perfect my ability to hold on to a mental image for a considerable length of time. He fixed his eyes on mine with a determined gaze in order to steady my vision to attention, but try as I might, I couldn't quite steady my gaze. A quick thought of the physical realm crept in and the moment was gone.

He just smiled, but I felt very disappointed that I had failed the exercise. We finished with him telling me that I would be with my future partner soon.

It was now summer again and I was approaching my thirty-fourth birthday. I had been enduring this alchemical process for almost a year and a half now but it was made clear to me that I was still not yet a clean vessel!

The next vision I had was very significant, indicating that it was again time for change. An unfamiliar entity with a beard, moustache and very wide face showed me a social setting at which a wine glass and two silver platters with grapes and other foods on were in view. He said, "Take your pick!"

I knew my phase of abstinence regarding alcohol and certain

foods was at an end.

In less than a month I would be linking up with a raven haired bachelor I had given a reading for two years back. We met over dinner with friends and he and I discussed how he too had been struggling with celibacy and had visited a meditation retreat for spiritual renewal. As we talked of various matters during the evening, I felt mysteriously drawn to him in a way that had not happened before.

I questioned things in my mind as our other dinner guests talked and I was puzzled by this influx of new energy. I was not risking any alcohol just yet either, even though it was now allowed, so I was completely sober. By the end of the evening I had a most bizarre feeling of having missed him deeply. So I decided to invite him along to my birthday gathering the following week.

This was the first occasion I was to have alcohol after my period of abstinence. I had vodka... along with champagne which was my favourite tipple in the past. I felt so lifted by the new energy and the fact that it was my birthday but I wasn't acting completely without caution. I had of course checked with The Great One and Ray beforehand that it was appropriate for me to date the bachelor.

A few days later I saw The Great One sitting in my heart centre. He was smiling with his eyes closed and communicated to me that I would soon be confirmed into a higher initiation. Two days later he fully manifested, pointed a sword at my heart and drew blood with its tip. He then lifted his right arm and pricked his inner elbow and wrist with the sword, but instead of blood, a brilliant light shot out through his arm and into my heart. The wound healed instantly and a seal was placed over it. I bowed my head in prayer and he told me I would feel a little pain where the ceremony had been performed. An hour or so later, I felt sharp pricking pains for a few moments and as I leaned forward, I heard him say "Receive Grace" and I felt a rush of energy through the back of my neck.

From then on I started to notice a distinct difference in taste and smell.

I went to visit the bachelor a few times and even stayed overnight at his place. One weekend however, he and I had joined some friends of his at a restaurant for dinner and to my shock and disappointment he ate meat in my company. Many people eat meat, of course, but now that I was dating him I thought he would settle for vegetarianism, as he knew I had been vegetarian since birth and he was aware of my views on the subject. I was so disgusted by his behaviour that I drank too much alcohol and ended up saying a few indiscreet things, rather regrettably. As upset with him as I was, I still felt very drawn to him and due to the indulgence in alcohol over the period of a few evenings, I ended up being intimate with him. I gave in to temptation.

I left the day after my faux pas at the restaurant and did not see him again for many months. I did not explain to him why I had to disengage. I just knew the energy had shifted between us. I returned home to my sanctuary and within a few hours I was to receive a devastating message."You were instructed to remain celibate".

It hit me like a sledge hammer. I was confused though, as I had definitely been given the sanction to date him. Spirit then made it clear to me that I had violated and spoiled the start of the relationship by breaking my vow of celibacy. I should have waited. It was my own stupidity. The bachelor was a gentleman and would have waited. I was riven with remorse and felt utterly downcast and was so truly sorry that I had misread the prompting and broken my vow but it was certainly not out of any malicious intent or conscious defiance.

The inner voice then sent through a message, "The battle in the psychic realms continues until it is won". Oh heavens, what could this mean now!

I saw my guide Miya once again after a long wait. She was sitting on the ground and mixing something in a bowl. She looked at me and said casually, "Don't worry yourself, you will put things right" and she lifted from her bowl the most beautiful piece of blue material.

It was now autumn and I was beginning to register messages coming from Ray by telepathic means. One night he appeared to me sitting in the lotus position and said, "Receive the flowers of acceptance". I couldn't help feeling that Ray, The Great One, and my guides were all disappointed in me. After all this time and the intense training, I had allowed myself to be influenced by my lower will. Once again I was told to limit my social life to mostly phone calls. I had thought about taking a trip to visit a girl friend in Thailand as I had not had a holiday since the previous year, but I was told it was not allowed and that I must wait and just keep praying and meditating. Thankfully, even after my error, I would still have moments of ecstasy and I came to seek this state more and more. I needed to surrender fully to be accepted by the Divine.

Instructions came from The Great One for me to call upon all my guides to a meeting during which they all sat round a large oval shaped table with The Great One at the head so to speak. I was kneeling on the floor whilst he was looking over as he discussed with my guides whether I was ready for him to turn the page in my life to the next chapter. I was hesitant at first but then spoke up and said that I was ready. He stared at me for a moment or two before turning the page and saying, "Believe me".

Oh yes, even now I still had my doubts, although they could be dispelled in an instant. I hoped with all my might that I could live up to what was expected of me.

I was giving thanks one evening to The Great One and my guides for all their patience and assistance, when boldly the words: "The Inner Healer comes" were shouted at me. I then saw myself flat on a floor facing upwards and a man swept a gush of energy over my body before raising me up in mid-air, as a large piece of cloth floated around me.

After midnight in a vision, The Great One stood facing me out in the open air with the blazing sun behind his head, watching the event. As I stepped towards him, demonic figures came at me from the ground and the sky. As startled as I was, I did not turn to run away and as I battled my way through, determined to reach him, I went straight through them and they vanished. When I finally reached him, I fell in his arms.

At first I was unable to fathom the depth of Ray's spiritual power. He disguised his humility so well and with my pride, the subtlest of my vices, I failed to grasp the full significance of the part he was playing in my spiritual training and unfoldment. I felt awful that I hadn't treated him with the honour and respect that he had so truly deserved. In comparison to me, my Teacher was a giant. The love I felt for him was so deep and innocent that words fail me in describing it. I prayed that on no account would I let my Teacher down, nor would I let The Great One, my guides or myself, down again.

CHAPTER 8

THE GREAT ONE'S INNER SANCTUM - FURTHER REVELATIONS

Things soon turned again when The Great One called me to "Come inside a little deeper". As I tuned in to his voice, I sensed dark forces coming near to the entrance I was approaching, but they quickly vanished and I entered a door that he sharply closed behind me, saying, "Don't worry about them". He then walked across the room and stared at me without speaking. He showed me a little grid on the floor and said, "See, it is in two pieces like most things". It looked to me like a puzzle that slotted together and as I pondered it, he spoke to me about phases of the moon.

I turned around and suddenly I found myself in what looked to be the Middle East and I became acutely aware of very different smells. I then saw a man whom I felt to be a Bedouin, shouting at a young boy and as I watched, he grabbed hold of the boy by the shoulder and shoved him in front of a mirror. As I focused in closely I saw that the boy was me. He had a slender frame, fine neck, black hair and very dark eyes with features somewhat resembling what I have now. For a brief moment I could feel myself in his skin. Then suddenly I was back in the room with The Great One.

This was to be the first of my visits to The Great One's holy place.

Just before the start of 2007 and during my usual opening up protection exercise before work, The Great One placed a robe around me, clasped it at the neck and said it was to be worn daily. That night I saw demonic entities but I was not afraid of them and I knelt to pray before The Great One.

He instructed me not to speak or think anything negative or

evil, as we are co-creators with the Divine and can literally create lower forces unbeknown to ourselves.

He added that surrendering to the Divine is the first step to transcendentalism and that to live a holy life one is to be graceful in speech, always surrender to the highest will and instruction, to be joyful, and to avoid being degraded by entertaining fear.

Days later I had a vision in which I saw myself stepping forward with my Teacher Ray, to bow before The Great One, who then proclaimed that, "The Real Life can only be taught here in this realm by a living example".

On a few occasions whilst I was in The Great One's presence I had seen and felt black slime coming from my mouth, but on this particular night as I was kneeling in silent prayer, I literally spat dirt out of my mouth.

A light quickly came and surrounded me and in bemusement I broke into tears. What was happening to me? The Great One's voice then shouted, "Come inside."

I heard the heavy door close and I was in a room with a stone floor that echoed. A large furnace was burning in the grate and I felt a little frightened so I started to say a prayer. In a flash I saw my body lying naked, flat on the floor facing upwards and I was quickly dragged through the furnace backwards. The flames were leaping all around me but they didn't burn me.

Then instantaneously, I was seated cross legged and the familiar omnipresent voice boomed "Let Me live in you".

I was suddenly transported to sitting just in front of the furnace and I had a little flame in the palm of each of my hands. The voice boomed again, "Do not be ignorant of Me or My powers."

I soon found myself back in my room with tears streaming down my face. I was petrified and unsure whether what I had just experienced was holy, so I rang my Teacher Ray. As I sobbed, he assured me that the experience was symbolic and that the two little flames represented streams of spiritual empowerment that I would come to use.

My spiritual education was stepping up a notch and more was explained to me about The Great One's abode, the forces in the air and how to use love on the in-breath.

After a peaceful meditation one evening, I saw The Great One with lightning reflected in his eyes and I knew that this meant trouble.

He said, "The holy hand that guides also provides. Stay still."

I immediately became aware of forces shooting overhead. I felt anxious, but then the forces dispersed, and he clasped my fingers and locked them in his and told me not to let go of his hand. As the scene calmed he said to me, "Why be concerned with what people think? Rather be concerned with what God thinks."

Afterwards I could smell roses everywhere.

After narrating the experience to Ray he suggested I go and buy some roses. So I went to do just that and on entering the shop, I saw a beautiful bunch of very large roses in a gorgeous cream colour. I felt immediately drawn to them but decided to look at some other roses too. I had only taken a couple of steps when spirit said to me clearly, "How seriously do you take your God?" I thought to myself, very seriously indeed, and walked directly back and picked up the bunch I had first been drawn to and to my amazement there was a reduced price sticker on them which hadn't been there seconds ago.

I took them home and put them in water and as I was arranging them I heard spirit say, "Law of seven = Godliness in Heaven. Law of three = Holiness on Earth".

I had no clue what this meant so I decided to quiz Ray about it. He seemed thrilled but didn't elaborate as to its meaning.

Later that day I found myself standing before an ancient looking man who was seated at an altar perusing notes. He spoke gently and said things about my health and work and then said, "You are beginning to understand and you will be judged well. You could have done better had you believed all you had heard. Now you believe you will do well indeed. You have passed; move on." And with that he shifted his attention back to his notes.

The weeks were flying by and I was soon to be receiving messages about world events on a frequent basis. I had even been shown tabloid and magazine headlines only to see them in print days later. I wondered what the point of such information was as I wouldn't be sharing the information with anyone, not even with my clients. Ray explained that this ability was proof that I was becoming able to function multidimensionally, transcending time and space.

I had also come to realize that to doubt and to question the teachings is to be expected from a sincere seeker, but doubt must be tempered with faith in the Divine and his messengers. Just because I could not always understand or believe something could be true, by no means meant that it was not true.

As spring was approaching, a very strange thing happened. My skin literally started to peel off, though it wasn't sore but was just flaking off. I went to my doctor who didn't seem to know why it was happening and he just suggested I use moisturisers, which I was already applying anyway. Rather embarrassingly, I told Ray about it, and he calmed me and explained that it was the turmoil I was enduring that was taking on an outer manifestation. I worried how long it might continue for and how this humiliating episode could be resolved. I decided to take salt baths until it healed.

The Great One called me in to his abode again and I was told to enter quickly and shut the door. Inside I saw the furnace again and started to panic. He said, "It won't burn you" and motioned for me to sit on the floor. I sat and put my feet close to the furnace and it felt warm.

He talked to me of many things and then marked my forehead with a symbol using the saliva from his mouth. I was told to live the Laws on the outside and the Path on the inside and also that the Laws can be taught outwardly but that the Path inwardly is unique to each, that each must be guided to the threshold of their own Path.

I had been doing some chores around the house one morning when suddenly in a flash I saw Sai Baba standing in my bedroom. He had bushy black hair and was shorter than I am. He placed some petals on each of my pillows and then he was gone. I didn't even know much about Sai Baba, so decided that after this visitation I should read up on him.

When I told Ray about it he said it was a wonderful manifestation and that Masters whether incarnate or discarnate, can materialize before a seeker who is making a determined effort towards attaining enlightenment, so as to cheer them on.

I remember reading a little book on Sri Yukteswar, who was the revered Teacher of Yogananda and could feel the force of this Master coming from his picture on the cover of the book.

It was astounding. On this same day I was clairaudiently given a message about one of the Prophets, containing details about his life when he was on earth. It surprised me a great deal but I was told not to discuss the subject with anyone, not even Ray.

I had also now begun to receive instructions and information on performing prayer rituals. Meanwhile, The Great One was ushering me into his abode much more regularly. I was later to discover that you cannot enter The Great One's abode by your own will unless you have made significant progress along the spiritual path.

On one occasion I was overwhelmed with feelings of ecstasy and felt drawn from the inside into an indescribable presence. I could feel my breathing to be flowing from my solar plexus and I registered a feeling of weightlessness and became one with everything around me.

The following night I was told I was 'Within the veil'. Ray was so happy for me and indicated that I had come so far that I must not look back now. A few days later I saw The Great One in his abode on his knees praying. I was stunned as I had never seen him in this way before. Ignorantly, I had assumed that he may be so advanced that he wouldn't need to pray. How foolish of me.

When I was getting ready for bed, I saw an outline of an entity coming up the stairs as I walked across the landing. I felt unnerved but decided to try and go off to sleep as normal. As I lay in bed with my eyes shut, I felt the entity come up close. I felt anxious and then The Great One's voice sounded and told me to open my eyes. With my heart thudding I did as instructed and stared at the hideous face looking at me. The Great One then told me to say some specific words and offer a prayer to the Divine, which I did, and the figure disappeared.

The following night I was to have my worst experience yet. I had woken up in the small hours after having a nightmare. As I tried to relax and settle back to sleep, I was suddenly dragged out of my bed by my ankles, and swung around in the air by what I took to be a negative entity. I had blurred vision and could not speak as I struggled, caught in its tremendous force-field. I tried with all my might to scream but no sound could come out of my mouth. I tried desperately to focus my thoughts on God. As I writhed, I eventually forced out a few specific words in the name of God and the second they were uttered, the entity dropped me instantly and I fell back on my bed as it disappeared.

I wondered if I had been deserted by my helpers in spirit as they had not stepped in. I was beside myself with hysteria and ran to the phone to call the only person I could, Ray. It wasn't yet dawn but I was desperate. As I heard his voice my hysteria intensified and I babbled, unable to string together a coherent sentence. He tried to console me and told me that learning not to distrust my guides, The Great One and Teacher, whenever I was threatened by an unpleasant experience was necessary, if I was to achieve enduring spiritual growth and awakening, without which I might fail in fulfilling the tasks that the Divine has allotted to me in the scheme of things.

I had no choice but to take counsel from my Teacher's encouragement . I resolved to welcome and learn from each individual manifestation that could descend upon me from the spiritual realm and to accept that what my helpers are expecting of me is to learn to transmute the negative forces that may assail me, into a beneficial flow of energy, using my mental resources.

My Teacher Ray sent me some Holy Ash after this ordeal and instructed me as to the specific places of the body I should apply it to. The morning after using the ash, I woke up to be greeted by an elderly lady in spirit with her arms outstretched towards me, calling me 'the little enchantress'. She said a few words about my future and then disappeared.

Another prompt came that afternoon with detailed information regarding a prayer ritual. It was then revealed to me that I could use the powers available to me to heal and to bless, under instruction. In prayer I asked if I could be cleansed on a daily basis from any negative thoughts I may have entertained.

The idea behind asking for this special grace was born during a conversation with Ray, who believes that we should not allow negative thoughts to build up, but aim to transmute them as we go along.

I decided I would ask for permission into The Great One's abode and to my surprise I was admitted. Once inside, I became as a child in height and appearance and instead of The Great One being present it was my guide HL. He was sitting on the floor and his hair looked so immaculately beautiful and shiny I could almost see my reflection in it. He welcomed me and began scooping a plentiful amount of very fine soft earth to his left. He shot me a quick glance and said, "Earthly goods". He then shovelled a large amount of the fine soft earth to his right and said, "Spiritual treasures". He then brushed his hands lightly together and with a smile said "Good. The accounts are settled," and added that from now on, I could ask for admittance at all times and it would be granted.

I then received a message to say that in three days time something significant would happen. Sure enough to my delight, after the third day my skin stopped flaking and instantly returned to its natural smoothness. Hurrah!

Early one morning, walking along an unfamiliar street with Ray, he told me he had a secret to share with me as we approached a large rather grand period house to attend a private meeting. I had learned by now that there was little use in quizzing him and that whatever he felt I needed to be told, would be conveyed to me in its right time and space.

Once inside in one of the large rooms, we joined a group of seven or so people, none of whom I knew. I seemed to be the youngest of those assembled and as I took a seat, one of the women came over to greet me and to give me some messages. I instantly felt uneasy in her presence and quite annoyed at some of what she had to say, as I felt it wasn't true and that she was in fact trying to provoke me. The room then emptied leaving just myself and two of the other women. Ray had also gone with the rest of the group, so I inquired where they had gone to and was told they had dispersed to other rooms in the house to talk amongst themselves.

As I looked around this fantastic room with its grand ceilings, I noticed a very beautifully dressed lady come and stand by the entrance wall. She appeared magnificent but had a mischievous air about her. It was silent and uncomfortable between us for a few moments and as I looked more closely at her face I realized she was the spirit of a most malevolent little girl, just in a woman's body. The very instant I saw through her facade, she lunged forward at me in a vicious attack and we got locked in battle. Her force was so strong that it was pushing me backwards as I tried desperately to stave her off with my arms. As the struggle continued, to my astonishment we began to lift off the floor; there was such hatred in her eyes, and she seemed to be actually enjoying this hideous drama.

I felt as if my arms would give way as we battled on up in the air close to the ceiling. I even feared she might overpower me as she did not seem to be weakening at all. I then began to repeat the name of the Divine over and over in my mind and tried to melt into that thought pattern. Slowly but surely a protective power then seemed to flow out of my head and through to her and finally this weakened her. Eventually we battled back onto the floor and the energy radiating from me pushed her back.

We then stood apart for a few moments staring at one another. She knew she had been beaten. She then changed suddenly in front of my eyes, into a small black dog and ran off to lie on the stairs just outside the room in the adjacent hallway, staring at me through the balustrades. I felt utterly sick and was so enraged, as well as out of breath that I was on the verge of tears. Within seconds, the other house mates came back into the room and to my utter astonishment no one even commented on the ruffled state I appeared to be in, or on the little black dog that was now on the stairs.

I had just about had enough by now, so I boldly approached the woman who seemed to have some authority in the house, telling her that I knew the dog was a malevolent little girl and I wanted to know what the heck was going on! She responded in a somewhat impartial tone that I had passed my test, although it didn't appear that she seemed pleased or wished to congratulate me at all. She just ushered me back to my Teacher Ray, who was now back in the other room.

When I spoke with him privately later on, I burst into tears, shouted and confessed that I wasn't sure if I could carry on with all this any more; the myriad tests of obedience that often made me feel as if I were on a torture rack were one thing, but this latest trial was something else. To my mind, things had got way out of hand and were now far far beyond normal. But he reassured me that I must not give up or look back now and reminded me that students on the path that turn back at this stage may lose out in their quest for spiritual illumination; since what seemingly are obstacles on the path, in a hidden way are a test to strengthen our mettle without which continuing progress and development might be hindered.

That day feeling exhausted, I performed a purification ritual using a special incense, and very late that night The Great One performed a ritual with me in his abode. He took something from my stomach area and covered me with a strange material. I was tired and he sat and watched over me, sitting in a very relaxed pose as he waited for me to fall asleep.

When I woke up it was morning and like a bolt out of nowhere the words "You Live" were shouted joyfully in my ears. I had now come to discover how to live in attunement with Divine will. I also heard the word "Vow" but I would have to wait to comprehend its full meaning, as well as realize that earth is a realm of contradictions.

In the past I had seen the odd glimpse of my previous incarnations and although they were intriguing and even shocking scenes, they had not as yet had a profound impact on me emotionally. But that was all about to change radically. I was soon to be shown a ceremony taking place in a large hall with a big staircase and many men lining the room. They seemed to be holding objects of some kind and in the centre of the floor, lying on a thin support, was a young slim woman. Her garments including a headdress were of the most exquisite colours. She looked so still I wondered if she may be dead. As I watched the scene unfolding, a tall and heavily built man began to raise her up on the thin support, very slowly and with great care, until she was in an upright position. She had been completely silent and had remained motionless up to this point but she then suddenly stepped forward and as she moved I knew I had been this lady in one of my previous incarnations a long time ago.

She proceeded to move gracefully and then stooped down to pick up a small animal from the floor, but to my horror and disgust, she bit into its neck with her teeth and killed it as part of the ghastly ceremony. I felt utterly sickened as I watched and tears filled my eyes. She then turned to one of the men who passed her a tiny infant that to my relief she cradled affectionately. I was unsettled for many days afterwards, as I loathed what had been done to the small animal.

It was growing warmer as it moved further into spring and on the whole I was feeling stronger than ever. I still had the odd pang of loneliness but many beautiful things were happening to me. My mother had shown up again to tell me about another celebrity I would be helping and she had come so close with such a warm smile on her face and had called me by my nickname. How happy I was to see her looking so well and moving on in spirit.

I had another past life vision and this was most unpleasant. I saw a middle aged woman in a long shabby skirt and white blouse, in a humble country cottage. The atmosphere was unsettled and charged with fear as I saw her run frantically into one of the rooms, quickly stuff some jewellery into her mouth and run out the back of her dwelling. Seconds later a soldier approached the place, found her, and pushed her violently to the ground. She fell face first in the mud and before she could make any attempt to escape, he pressed his foot down on her back and with a clean swoop cut off her head with his weapon before taking her precious jewels. The woman was me. I had felt her fear and emotions so deeply that I was left feeling shaken for some time.

The awful headaches I used to have were less frequent these days, but on this particular evening I felt as if there was a heavy clamp on my head again, so I decided to go to bed early hoping to sleep it off, but it just got more painful.

I had been lying with my head sunk in the pillows for a time when I heard The Great One speak gently. He lifted what seemed to be strips of energy off my back, neck and shoulders and soon I felt lighter and sleepy. He spoke again and said, "Don't fall asleep yet, I have something to tell you" and he shared something about my path.

When I awoke in a few hours it wasn't yet dawn. As I opened my eyes and focused, I saw The Great One instantly and he said happily "New beginning".

I then fell into a mystical rapture and heard a voice, concerning my spiritual life, which seemed to come from a Divine presence. I felt so happy I could have burst.

The Great One then showed me many things concerning my future work and told me that Ray would at some point in the future take a back seat, that this was his own wish, but that the link between my Teacher and me was eternal and would not be undone. He went on to say how highly advanced Ray is and that he would carry on in his own way.

The Divine voice boomed again, "You are not a saint but your work is for Me, commune with Me daily."

I was then led through a healing ritual by The Great One and then led into a small room, where a Spiritual Being who appeared to be male but not human, was busy working. He responded respectfully to The Great One and carried on with his duties. The Great One then continued, "You have passed and you are with me" and before I could thank him with all my heart, he went on to explain that for laws to be understood and lived, you must be tested in your own way as I had been. He added that I must wait now for the next phase and that he had to go just then. I asked him if I could still join him 'Inside' if I wished and he said "You are free".

From this point on each state of prayer ushered in considerable bliss.

Soon after I was using my letter cards and they whizzed out to spell the word 'Chela,' which I came to learn after looking them up, meant an aspiring disciple .

A few days later, Ray phoned and said in his usual half laughing lilt, "If one is to become a disciple of The Path, Cher, it means a lot of work. You have been warned."

I had not even told him what my letter cards had spelled out.

Next, I found myself in a state of trance and I recall being rolled up by The Great One like a small ball, while he pasted a thick oily substance in the shape of a symbol I couldn't recognize onto the back of my neck. I was told by him that the sign was a mark of recognition signifying my spiritual progress. When I next spoke with my Teacher Ray, he confirmed The Great One's words, adding that I was being prepared for very special spiritual tasks for the future and that my gifts would grow to further heights.

Shortly afterwards I was shown two further past life clips, in between giving readings for clients one afternoon. One of the clips revealed who Ray was in a previous incarnation and how he had helped me in that lifetime. The second one was a scene of me in a previous life as a man in my sixties, dressed in a religious ceremonial garb and writing away with an old fashioned writing implement.

This revelation was followed by a voice issuing from a Divine presence, "I am your Source and your Force, your Foresight and your Insight. Your co-workers have laboured hard and will support you. Alchemy is the gold that cannot be bought, the price that cannot be paid except with life itself."

In April, Whitey my other male guide whom I had not seen for ages, came to me and told me I must relax my view of people and be more tolerant but not to compromise spiritual values and the Laws of the Inner Path; he admonished me that I was to be more gentle when helping and teaching others.

Soon after I felt an energy come into the room. As I looked up, I saw an evil little entity approaching me. I found myself smile at it calmly as I was moved with pity but without harbouring any fear. As it slowly walked away, I sensed that some of the negativity it had been radiating had disappeared. Ray commented on this experience adding that lower entities sometimes draw close to the inner light of a seeker, so as to be aided on their own journey to the Divine.

Still in April, I had the experience of gently entering into the body of The Great One, as if I was a ball of light! He told me that he had been with me in times past, guiding me towards holiness. I then found myself at a table with him and my guides and as they spoke of the work ahead, a narrow band of rays came down into the middle of the table.

The next day before I started work, The Great One put the cloak on me and it looked as if it was dripping with gold. He glanced at me with a smile and said, "Spiritual gold."

And then like nectar I was to be given a message that would send my soul soaring with joy: "The Divine is pleased with your work". I was ecstatic and that night, the omnipresent voice sounded, "The freedom I have given you is priceless."

I had gone once again to meditate with the older gentleman Ed and during the session I went inside The Great One as pure energy and was shown many things; including Ray, my Teacher, sitting in the midst of a small group of people. As I tuned in closer to see things in more detail, I recognized one of the men as Yeshua but was not permitted to see who the other highly evolved beings were in the group.

When I later told Ray whom I had seen him with, he just said "okay" and didn't elaborate at all. Set on wanting to know more, I persisted with the subject and asked if he may have abilities like Yeshua. I was curious to know why I had seen him with the Prophet and who the others were, as I was aware Ray was non denominational in his views. But he just said it was blasphemous for me to speak such things and it was left at that.

When I was next preparing before starting work, a symbol was marked on my cloak and The Great One said to me, "One can only be blessed when one is blessing someone else". It then seemed as if the flood gates had opened and I was filled with Divine peace. "You can only share what you have and thus only have what you share" were the words that sounded.

Hours later, I was sitting in between The Great One and my Teacher Ray, like an ant between two giants. They were discussing things together and as I looked on, a soldier in uniform went to The Great One's side and spoke with him privately for a few moments. I wondered what was going on, when he answered me and said that other people needed his assistance and permission too. It hadn't even occurred to me that The Great One would be helping lots of other people as well who were trying to work closely with him as I was. My view was nowhere near to fully panoramic yet.

Following this experience I heard the word "Bodhisattva" which is a Buddhist term for a Great One who chooses to continue to reincarnate on earth until all beings have attained enlightenment!

It was now mid May 2007 and the sun was shining, so I sat outside to soak up a few rays before working. Within minutes I could faintly see a form coming into view and as it became clear, I saw that it was a dark feathered bird staring right at me. I was informed clairaudiently as I focused on it that it had come to thank me from the bird kingdom. I was so shocked and thought it utterly bizarre that I laughed. When I decided to share it with Ray, he said that it was wonderful and that all beings including animals, have their Collective Group Spirits and how these mould the plant and elemental kingdoms into the manifold forms in which we see them.

I was in the shower later that week when The Great One's voice called out, "The walls of your ego have been smashed and the demons have been fought" and after a pause he said "No slacking" and then something was revealed about Interplanetary Love. I knew nothing of Interplanetary Love previously.

Since February, I had been back in touch with the raven haired bachelor whom I had broken my celibacy vow with. I felt strongly that I should at least give him an explanation of sorts and tentatively tried my best to hint at the mistake I had made by taking things too far with him; that if I had waited things may have worked out for us. I didn't go into any details regarding my esoteric experiences.

It had been made clear to me again in no uncertain terms, that I should remain celibate and impartial and not date anyone, not even for dinner until it was sanctioned for me to do so.

My Teacher Ray had also warned me to expect the unexpected, as The Masters could change anything at any moment (with Divine sanction). He told me of a wonderful story of a very Great Master who was destined to be born on earth and that two sets of parents in different countries had been pre-selected for him to be born to, but the powers that be left the decision opaque to everyone including the Great Master himself, until the very last moment; and just as it seemed as if it was going to be the parents in one country, it was switched and he was to be born to the other set of parents in the other country.

The next batch of what I term as 'psychic post' (whereby information is just delivered to me without my asking for it), was very detailed indeed and this contained private information concerning a wealthy and respected family that I had met. The information was extremely clear as to their wealth having been built on fraud and theft. Information included that the female head of the family had been dreadfully unhappy since the birth of her second child and that her husband had been involved with another woman. I was astounded and wondered why I should need to know of such things. I did my best to remain non-judgmental and kept it discreet since spirit had warned me that even some of the family members themselves were not aware of such details.

One morning I was woken up to be told to "Make a

commitment to the Divine". I didn't really understand the message, as to my mind I was already committed to the Divine. How could my life possibly be any more committed to the Divine than it was now? Then I was told again, "Make a commitment to the Divine, a mark to remind you of your spiritual life".

I was confused, so I went and sat in my garden for clarification and sure enough, after a while it came. During these few special moments, a further part of my contract with the Divine was revealed and there and then, I agreed to adhere to it fully.

As the month drew to a close, Ray was to enlighten me a little more regarding the laws of karma including how the denizens and hidden forces of this realm operate. He shared with me that his own Teacher was able to transmute some of another person's karma, if the Divine willed it and if the person deserved it. I told him that I had heard that Sai Baba was also able to do this and he smiled at me with a glint in his eyes and said, "In future you will move towards being able to do this too."

I was speechless, as I couldn't imagine myself becoming so evolved as to be able to transmute other people's karma. I also wondered what type of initiations, tests, paradoxes and sacrifices, attaining this level of spiritual advancement would require. Ray then added that it would soon be time for me to start living a family life in this world.

Ray and I discussed the issue of diet many times. We are both vegetarians but he had tried on various occasions to suggest to me to be tolerant of those who eat meat out of necessity. A few years back, I had been given a very clear and direct message from spirit that "People are not to eat animals as if they are fruit" and I couldn't agree more.

Since each and everyone is connected with the universal mind which is all-knowing, it stands to reason that any single act or event occurring at any place, no matter how distant, can be revealed to us by the indwelling soul through dreams, clairvoyant images and promptings from within if we are deemed deserving by the cosmic intelligence.

I will share a brief story that concerns a male friend (let me call him Mr Jones) who was destined to have revealed to him his female partner's liaison with a third party. Mr Jones was driving through his home town when as he stopped at some traffic lights, he noticed a huge board mounted up on an old closed down shop window. On the board, Mr Jones saw inscribed his strange christian name. He thought this odd as he had driven past the shop many times before but had not noticed the board. The traffic lights changed and he drove off to carry out his business. On completion of the errands, Mr Jones felt inclined to drive back and take a closer look at the shop window and the board showing his christian name. He got to the destination parked his car, and walked towards the shop. There was a little restaurant close by that he knew of very well. It was early evening and there were not many customers eating in the restaurant. He was prompted to turn his gaze towards one of the huge adjoining restaurant windows. To his shock and disappointment there sat inside was his female partner with an accompanying male friend. He could not believe his eyes. Mr Jones did not have the heart to go into the restaurant to confront his partner. He moved back towards the shop but could not find the board with his christian name and wondered who had put up the board initially.

The timing of the whole event was very significant. Synchronicity was what was at work. If he had stopped to take a closer look earlier in the day when he had first seen the sign on the board through the window, the man would not have been sitting in the nearby restaurant with his partner. Mr Jones confronted her later that evening when she was back at home and she confessed.

I also knew of an acquaintance who had a contemplative and religious turn of mind by nature. He went to bed one night and was literally shown in a dream that his wife was in love with another man; and added to this information, he was shown the actual appearance of his wife's lover. He was so moved by the clarity of his dream that at breakfast, he asked his wife outright if she was in love with another man. She was stunned and wondered how and where he could possibly have obtained the information. She confessed there and then, overwhelmed by the sheer accuracy of the dream. The married man was deemed deserving of Divine beneficence.

Our attunement with the universal mind never ceases. Through it, information relevant for our spiritual unfoldment will always be channelled through to us as we each continue on the path towards Divine illumination.

One sunny afternoon in June, as I lay outside in my conservatory to relax after work, a series of visions came flooding in and information was conveyed to me as to how to send out help instantly and telepathically to people, beings, and places, as and when instructed. As I followed the prompts that came, I saw my thought patterns take form as I sent out help.

A little later, I had a 'visitation' from an older Indian lady who told me she is living on earth and presently working in a certain part of India. She told me that she blesses infants by gently holding them in her arms and blowing on them softly, using a particular breathing technique. She added that she can also heal.

The experience was wonderful and if we should ever meet in person, I am sure we will recognize each other and share our esoteric knowledge.

I woke up the next day feeling recharged and happy, but before I could even get out of my bed I heard out loud, "You killed someone".

I was horrified and tried to gather my thoughts, but a scene then unfolded in front of my eyes. I saw a house and a watermill and close by stood a man with a hat on and a light coloured beard, looking a bit dishevelled and desperately worried. I saw fields in the distance and then my focus shifted to the large wheel of the mill which was turning slowly and as it came round I could see the figure of a dead woman in a blue dress. My focus then shifted to the man again and as soon as I caught his eye, I knew he was 'me' in a life before. He seemed deeply frightened and troubled. Then the scene faded. I couldn't be certain if he had killed the woman by accident or not? I just hoped it had happened by mistake. I felt sick and dejected.

When I told Ray about it, he just laughed and reminded me that everyone is here on earth to polish up and make up for past errors. So feeling a little more inspired, I got on with my plans for the day and took the train to the city to meet the older gentleman Ed for meditation. As the ticket inspector approached me on the train, he seemed unable to hear what I was saying to him. To my bewilderment and embarrassment I had to shout at him three times before he could hear me. It was incomprehensible to me, as I knew he had heard the other passengers in the carriage, who were now staring and laughing at me, perfectly well. Then on my arrival at Charing Cross station, I popped into one of the shops to buy a few items and the same thing happened with the cashier. Even though I was speaking to the cashier face to face, he seemed not to be able to hear the words coming out of my mouth, even though by now I was speaking quite loudly. I felt that something strange was going on and that I was possibly in an invisible bubble that was soundproof.

Needless to say Ray laughed when I told him and he said I was being sheltered by an invisible protective shield and that spiritual Masters on earth, if they choose, can literally walk amongst crowds and remain unnoticed and invisible to the gaze of people around them.

As the days unfolded in July, I felt more and more neutral, not just about my psychic pressures and responsibilities but even regarding my personal life. I was achieving balance.

A few weeks prior to my thirty-fifth birthday, I woke up in the early hours. I was soaked through with sweat, my body and hair were wringing wet.

I heard, "All in one night" and I knew that much of my karma had been worked through. I felt so empowered and invigorated that the next day I became deeply happy and blissful.

A few hours later, my Teacher Ray phoned to say, "The Holy Ones have promoted you, Cher," with a little laugh, he likened what I had been enduring to SAS style training. He also added that I may be told at some point in the future to stop giving readings for people, which surprised me a great deal, but he went on to say that my spiritual work would continue in a variety of ways.

Lately my journeying into other realms has taken a splendid turn. It will suffice for me to say that I have on occasion been admitted, as a junior, to places too glorious to accurately describe. On one such visit, I entered a place to go and worship and was met by a highly evolved being who appeared non-human. He taught me a certain word, that when uttered with spiritual authority, allows attunement with higher powers.

The Great One has said to me recently that I am to consider being a partaker of the burdens of humanity, as a blessing from the Divine.

The last time I saw my Teacher face to face, he postulated that the Divine created everything, both good and evil, and that the purpose of human evolution, is for us all to progress by learning to integrate and harmonize the two opposing forces through self-realization; and thereby achieve union with the Godhead.

CHAPTER 9

SELF HELP AND DEVELOPMENT

Introduction

In my work as a spiritual adviser and medium, I meet people from all walks of life who may be aiming to awaken their inner psychic potential through the use of prayer, mental disciplines involving concentration and meditation; as well as ritualistic acts such as the burning of incense, candles and special herbs universally considered as being sacred.

I often say to my clients that it is not wrong to pursue psychic development and the powers it confers such as inner visioning and hearing and the ability to heal people from a distance.

Indeed, I sometimes suggest or teach techniques for exploring the inner dimensions of spirit which is what psychic development entails.

However, I usually counsel those who consult me to approach the subject with the purest of motives since all psychic gifts are ultimately bestowed via the grace of the Universal Intelligence. To use or apply knowledge selfishly or with the aim of harming someone could adversely affect one's spiritual growth, bring immediate harm or even weaken the inherent ability of a practitioner to ward off or transmute oppositional influences marauding in the eternal realms.

I will share with you an incident that happened in my life when I was only seventeen . I had been working as a model for a short while and had found an agent in London to plan my professional activities.

Since I was quite young, I did not appreciate how much the power of thought, if projected and directed to a self-created mental image, can influence the outcome of an event. I was meant to be getting a lift up to London for a photoshoot, from a female friend and her partner. I had to be in London very early in the morning and the train from where I lived could not have got me there in time and as yet I could not drive, so they had kindly offered to take me. I just had to make my way to their place so as not to delay the trip. I made sure that I was early but I waited and waited for their planned arrival. We did not have mobile phones back then or I did not anyway; perhaps the odd yuppie would have a phone the size of a brick in his car but that was all. Anyway, as I stood there in the morning air and time ticked on, it began to occur to me that they had left without me on purpose, out of spite, as I felt the girlfriend was jealous of me because of my achievements, modest though these were. The moment I realized this to be true, in an angry flash I directed my thought to them and pictured them in a car crash.

I was so upset as I made my way to a phone box to call my agent to tell him there was no way I would be able to make it to the photoshoot in time. He wasn't the least bit pleased, of course, as it was at such short notice. My ego was flattened and I went home. Later that evening, I called my girl friend to confront her about why they had left without me since they knew full well how important the photoshoot was to me, and that they were my only means of getting up to London at that hour in the morning. She was a little shaken and upset and told me that en route, they had been involved in an accident and had to abandon their trip but that they were very much shaken but not hurt.

I put the phone down white as a sheet, of course, not having mentioned the angry thought I had so powerfully directed towards them both. I felt awful and extremely scared at what I had played a part in. I did not really think or fully know that it could happen. I had reacted negatively and spontaneously believing they had hurt and let me down on purpose. Who was the jealous and guilty party here? After this my friendship with my female friend dwindled dramatically. Many years later, I bumped into her and she apologized for having been so jealous of me. Needless to say, I silently extended to an old friend and fellow pilgrim a charitable hand of friendship.

A Protection Technique
The mind may lead a seeker to utter confusion on the path and in extreme cases even a momentary loss of one's mental balance. The labyrinths of the inner worlds need to be explored with not only the right motive but also with spiritual protection.

Sadly it is fairly common for people interested in psychic development to just go and buy themselves a pack of Tarot cards or try experimenting with Ouija boards, without any prior training, experience or protection to speak of. Many times I have read for people who think that the spirit shifting things in their house and saying rude things to them is their Spirit guide!

There are many protection exercises that one can use but I will just focus on a very simple and effective one. It may also be performed discreetly in a matter of seconds and so is very useful if you are in a crowd or out in a public place even.

Close your eyes for a few moments and take your inner focus to your third eye Chakra, between the eyebrows. Visualise white light coming clearly in to view and gently allow it to completely envelop you like a ball of light covering your entire being. Then send your thoughts high telepathically and ask The Divine or your Spirit guides and angelic helpers to keep you protected.

I might add here that if you may be harbouring any negative resentment or ill will to anyone and have not yet forgiven and released it, your own levels of protection may be lessened since thoughts that are negative eat into our own inner goodness.

A Prayer Technique for Guidance
To pray is to aim to enter into communion with the Divine and this could be done silently as happens during meditation or

through a verbal recitation of a written prayer.

I consider it a form of prayer whenever I focus on The Divine, throughout the day whilst going about my business. I don't feel it necessary to be in a specific place to engage in prayer. One may feel drawn into spiritual attunement at any time, and anywhere.

I do of course carry out very specific prayer rituals if and when I am instructed to. And these types of rituals may help us all to deepen and expand our spiritual life.

I have to say that I feel it is just as important to sit silently after prayer and wait for a response; otherwise it seems more like talking at or asking The Divine for assistance and or answers without allowing the time and opportunity for feedback. Too many people pray and then just carry on with their daily routine or if at night, go straight to sleep. I feel that what The Divine may have to reveal or say to us is far more important than what we may have on our wish list. Wait for a response in silence!

When you can find time, sit quietly, you may light a candle if you wish, and breathe as deeply and slowly as possible with your eyes and mouth closed. Try not to focus just yet on your prayer or wish list requests, just allow the feelings upwelling from within travel to The Divine. Allow your heart to speak. If then you feel the need to speak or put in a specific request, do so.

Wait afterwards for at least a few minutes in silence. Close with thanks.

Gratitude is a key ingredient in spiritual development. If you have a serious or specific problem you need assistance with, then repeat the process with the same request for three nights in a row.

Healing

Professional healers apply a variety of techniques to channel healing energies to their clients. I have had no formal training as a healer. The two approaches I have often used are absent healing and hands on healing as taught by my spirit guides and angelic helpers. They have also taught me that it is not always right for people to assume that to be healed is a 'good' thing. My guides believe that someone who is suffering in some way at a certain point in their evolutionary journey may be benefiting from the experience and learning valuable lessons to aid their soul growth; and that to take that suffering away from them may well impede their spiritual advancement. I reason that each person's fate is unique according to the karmic law of cause and effect into which our lives are interwoven, and following from this principle, that one must seek guidance and permission from higher intelligences before proceeding with spiritual healing.

Absent Healing Technique

It is preferable to do this exercise on an empty stomach, not after you have had a heavy meal.

To start with, quieten the mind, take a few deep breaths and use your inner focus to visualize a protective sheath of white light surrounding you. Then allow your thoughts to flow out to the Divine and ask for guidance while building up a clear image of the person requesting assistance.

Wait before proceeding any further. If you surrender your own will to the Higher Mind and remain silent a prompt of some kind will come from within.

Depending on your level of spiritual attunement, an answer may be given to you clairaudiently or else an empowering and positive flow of energy may touch you and beckon you on to proceed.

If either of these pointers are absent it is best to leave the process for now. Timing is sacred.

Assuming a clear prompt has come for you to assist, then humbly consider acting as a vessel or channel through which the healing energies from the higher invisible realms can flow and connect with the person you are assisting. Picture them clearly in your mind's eye and petition The Divine for the highest outcome.

The exercise need not take more than five minutes. Usually in my experience, I am told what to do, which of the energy centres of the person to focus on; and at the end of it all the words 'It is done' meaning my part is complete will resonate to my inner hearing. Close the event by giving thanks to The Divine or the angelic helpers or guides you worked with.

Hands On Healing Technique

I would only recommend that hands on healing be carried out by someone who had been given professional training by another healer or by angelic helpers and guides in spirit.

I have often been told to assist people by placing specified crystals or my hands on certain parts of a person's body. The Great One and some of my guides and helpers have been present at the healing session to assist me. I just follow instructions and prompts. Sometimes the person receiving healing has an inner vision and bliss as the healing energies were getting to work. Occasionally, the client feels pain as negative energy is shifting.

So again, assuming permission has been given for you to assist, begin by quietening the mind.

Take a few deep breaths and ask for Divine protection, for a few minutes before entering the room of the person you are going to assist. Then ask The Divine for the highest outcome before applying the technique. When you are prompted to complete the session, leave some water for the client to drink. Then quietly leave the room for a few minutes to allow them to adjust and bring their focus back to this dimension. Close down the session and give thanks to The Divine and any guides and helpers who have assisted.

Cleansing the Aura and Energy Centres or Chakras

As with the other healing exercises, firstly quieten the mind, take a few deep breaths and visualize that you are being protected by beneficent intelligences.

Aim your thought to The Divine and ask for guidance and the highest outcome. If and when the sanction is given, proceed as prompted or instructed.

For this exercise you may use incense or ideally red sage. The red sage should be completely dried out so it is almost crispy. Take a few small sprigs and break them up in a small heatproof bowl.

The client should be seated comfortably with a straight back, preferably on a chair in the centre of the room, so as to enable you to move freely around them.

Caution: If at any time you feel or you are prompted to stop, then you must do so immediately. I was once using the red sage cleansing technique to help a gentleman and was suddenly told mid-way through the session to 'stop' and that the man was not ready yet to go any deeper.

As I brought him out of the trance-like state he said,

"Thank goodness you stopped! I felt as if I would fall off my chair and I could see other people in the room but not clearly". Red sage cleansing is a powerful ritual. The properties of the herb can induce a trance-like but relaxed state triggering inner visioning and empowerment.

Assuming the client is ready to undergo the aura cleansing exercise, then light the dried red sage in the bowl and once it is smoking, blow out the flame, just as you would with incense. Then circle slowly around the client's seven energy centres (chakras) starting from the root chakra at the base of the spine through to the sacral, the solar plexus, the heart and throat chakras respectively, the third eye chakra between the eye brows and finally the crown chakra at the top of the head, gently allowing the red sage smoke to billow around the energy centres.

Once complete it is often wise, unless prompted otherwise, to gently place your hands on the client's feet to ground them.

Then close the ritual offering thanks to The Divine, angelic helpers and guides. Allow the person to remain seated silently for at least five minutes before gently bringing their focus back to this dimension and offering them water to drink.

Transmuting Negative Memories, Energies and Invoking Forgiveness

This next technique may be used to achieve empowerment so as to forgive those who have wronged you. It may also be applied for transmuting and releasing locked up negative energies.

You will need one heatproof bowl, a second bowl for water, clean white paper and a pen.

Begin with the usual protective visualization technique. Take a few deep breaths and ask The Divine for the highest outcome.

Firstly, visualize yourself being protected and take a few deep breaths. Then tear or cut the white paper into strips and on each individual piece write down the emotional feeling you wish to release. Try and keep to one word per strip of white paper. For example, if you wish to release anger and forgive just write the word anger on one strip. Then on another strip of white paper write the name of the person you wish to forgive or the event that you may be angry about.

When you feel you have written down every emotional issue you wish to release, place the strips in your heat proof bowl and burn them. When all the pieces have turned into blackened ash, water being a purifier, pour water into the bowl.

Close with thanks to The Divine.

Remote Viewing

It is possible to learn what is there to be discovered or known about a distant place or locality far removed in respect of time and space through Remote Viewing. This technique calls for the use of inner visioning (clairvoyance) and inner hearing (clairaudience).

Remote Viewing comes into play during absent healing and also when one is asked to conduct a psychic investigation of a haunted property not close by. We all have gifts which are unique but if you think you have the appropriate psychic abilities and you aim to engage in Remote Viewing then as usual ask The Divine for protection, guidance and permission if a client or some one in need approached you for assistance.

If and when sanctioned, focus your inner view on the specific place or person and respectively names, addresses and geographical location; also ask an individual's date of birth.

Once locked into the energy pattern of the place or person, you should be able to 'see' and look around to explore the location and even 'see' what the person may be doing; and if you are clairaudient, you will be able to 'hear' what is being said.

Many things may be observed and heard in this way and the remote viewer must act with the utmost discretion and responsi-bility revealing only as much as they are allowed, to avoid being held to account by the universal law of justice and compensation. The karma price tags to be paid for using these gifts frivolously are very heavy.

Meditation Technique

Since meditation entails opening up mentally into the invisible realms, who we choose to meditate with is very important. This is because these realms throw up not only pleasant but also unpleasant flows of vital energies. To my mind it is better to meditate alone than with others who may not have the right motive.

It is true that meditation may lead to the unlocking of hidden psychic faculties but this should not be the main objective, ideally the motive of a seeker should be rooted in spiritual progress. The psychic faculties will unfurl if and when they are destined to.

In my early years, when I was first introduced to the disci-plines of meditative practice in Ben's circle, I was taught initially to focus on the flame of a candle positioned in the middle of a darkened room. With my eyes open and concentrating on the little flickering flame, I learned (eventually) to still the incessant chatter of my conscious mind. Each time my monkey mind had me trailing off thinking about anything and everything under the sun, I would as quickly as possible stop the train of thought and focus again on the candle flame. I was training my mind to shut up!

As I progressed I could then sit with my back straight in a chair, with eyes closed and still mind, go into silent meditation. A 'gap' started opening up in the vacuous spaces of my mind's eye allowing me to travel at will into the infinite realms of the invisible.

If you are already a lone practitioner, I would suggest that you create a sacred space as an initial act by visualising yourself within a circle of white light. Simultaneously, tune in to the Universal Intelligence and aim to share the spiritual gains that will be bestowed on you with all of your fellow pilgrims. Sit upright with your back straight (if you lay down you may fall asleep!).

Breathe gently and deeply with your eyes closed (you may find the exercise relaxing) and try to master the chatter of the mind. Focus inwardly on each of your seven energy centres or chakras beginning with the root chakra at the base of the spine, work your way up through each chakra, the sacral, solar plexus at the navel, the heart and the throat chakras, and the third eye chakra positioned in between the eye brows and finally to the crown chakra positioned at the top of the head.

Continue to sit still for about half an hour and in a silence, wait for The Divine to commune with you and close with deep gentle breathing before opening your eyes.

CHAPTER 10

APPLYING THE GIFTS – INTRODUCTION AND CASE STUDIES

On average I help more than twenty people per week. Every case is unique just as everyone is unique, but obviously, there are some general problems that lots of people experience. When it comes to helping various individuals who have contacted me on their own initiative, I am able to pick up and relay to them valuable information from spirit. All a medium need do is to focus on a person's name, date of birth, photograph or just the voice vibration of the individual. I consider it unethical however, where a gifted psychic out of curiosity stretches out to pry into the hidden life of another person without permission.

This 'Psychic theft' is not the same as what I term 'Psychic post' where a medium is quite literally delivered information regarding anyone, anything or even world events. I have been in situations where I may be sitting with people, at dinner for instance, when information will just be dropped in to my mind as to how those particular individuals have made their wealth, had illnesses, lost a child or if there's someone in the group who happens to be having an affair. This 'psychic post' is usually followed by "Shh" if it is meant to remain unmentioned.

A few years ago, a group of people came to me with very similar problems. All of them had lost loved ones in very mysterious, violent or tragic circumstances. A lot of information came through as I read for them but I did not always feel comfortable tuning in to what had happened in their lives. I then wondered if I was being tested by a certain organisation regarding my abilities, as I had once received a message through my answering machine, asking me to contact a particular person on a certain number if I was interested in working for an organisation specializing in forensic investigation. I was not interested in pursuing this line of work so I did not call them. But there are gifted mediums and psychics who specialize in such cases and work with forensic experts.

Giving messages to assembled individuals from a platform in the spiritualist church years back, in the end gave me great confidence. I recall sitting behind a little curtain while the place began to fill with people hoping to hear from a loved one, or to get a clip of information concerning the future. I felt so nervous that I said to my guide Winn, "This is up to you, if you don't speak I won't have any messages to give!"

Acting on higher instructions in the course of helping clients, does not mean that people will always be easy to advise or even grateful for the advice they hear. What goes for one person may not necessarily apply to another since individual destinies vary greatly here on earth.

As a medium, I can aid those who approach me to link up with their loved ones in spirit, as well as uncover the hidden truths in their lives which may have a bearing on their existential problems. I only act as a facilitator. I avoid as much as I can encroaching on others free will, a Divine endowment of a client, as this could short-cut and endanger a person's evolutionary unfoldment.

Also we don't just sprout angelic wings when we pass over into spirit, we still have to evolve in other realms as we do here on earth.

The following case studies are meant to show how I have been using the gifts to assist people from various walks of life. My clients include artists, celebrities, lawyers, ordinary working men and women, musicians, housewives, entrepreneurs, prostitutes, medics, physicists, bankers, civil servants, other mediums and healers, architects, farmers, make-up artists, actors, teachers, estate agents, traders, soldiers, sports men and women, models and so on.

I have also worked on TV shows with other mediums and psychics and have performed psychic investigations at different locations such as castles, stately homes, celebrities houses and some well known haunted historic sites for a national newspaper.

Needless to say, confidentiality is a top priority in my work and for this very reason I will not be disclosing the names and identities of my private clientèle.

Case Studies

Ask And You Will Receive
I read for a beautiful young lady named Eleanor who had come to me regarding some difficulties she was having in her turbulent love life. She said she needed guidance in relation to a specific question that she wanted answering. I explained to her that we could ask and see, but that it was up to my guides and ultimately the Divine whether an answer could be given to her. And so the question was asked and to my surprise an answer was given and it happened to be the answer she now admitted she had been hoping for. She was very excited suddenly and asked me if I could try and ask again just to make sure the answer was correct. I was apprehensive as I knew my guides would wonder if I was doubting them. Anyway I asked again. She was so happy to hear that the first answer had been correct, and was so ecstatic that she asked again; "Are you positive?" and I just thought she was pushing her luck too far and before she even got around to suggesting that we ask a third time, spirit actually spoke out loud and broke the sound barrier for her to hear "Try that again, please". The young lady leapt up from her seat and ran out through the back door of the house screaming and crying. I went after her to comfort her of course, trying not to laugh too much

and it was some time before she asked me to read for her again. Just to be clear on the matter; the answer given was proved correct and manifested a short time soon after.

Honesty Rewarded

A very tenuous family situation was once relayed to me by Lee, a lady who was so confused that she was not even sure if she wanted her partner, who had recently left the family home, to return. Her unsettled state of mind had led her into a silly affair with a man she knew was unsuitable and whom certainly did not want to be responsible for her and her children. By the time she came to ask for my help, she truly believed that her partner would not come back.

I was given very clear information as to how to assist her and was even told to use a candle and perform a little prayer ritual for her family as a whole. I explained to her that to restore the spiritual balance and to achieve a lasting bond with her partner, she would have to admit to him everything about the affair as well as any other matter that she was unhappy about concerning her partner.

She was not in the least bit happy to hear that she had to come clean but I told her that if she wanted her family to start afresh and go forward together in the coming years, then she must make a sacrifice and endure the humiliation of admitting to her partner to having been selfishly used by another man for sex in an affair.

She finally found the courage to tell her partner and although he was unhappy at first, he felt sorry for her and forgave her. They reconciled and years on, they are still together.

Can Fate Be Avoided

Back in the days when I would read for clients face to face, a man named Daryl came to see me one day whilst I had a female friend visiting. I let him in although I was not alone since I felt it was safe to do so. He said that he had heard of my psychic abilities, but that he wasn't entirely convinced of things of that nature but wondered if I might be able to read for him anyway.

I felt he needed help even though he only half believed and I said I would try and link up with spirit for him. I did not tune in and open up in front of him, but instead had a look at his planetary alignment from his date of birth as he sat opposite me, using an astrology book my mother had given to me. As I began to look at his planet positions, information just started to flow through.

I told him that he was secretly very frightened about going to prison for something he had done that no one else knew about. He immediately started to fidget in his chair. His eyes widened and he became very nervous when a few more details came up regarding his family life, partner and children and the other women he had seen in the past. He became frozen like a statue as he just stared at me but then something happened which I had not yet experienced before.

I was shown a complete blank clairvoyantly concerning his future and a total void descended upon the path that lay ahead for him. I was not sure what to say to him, so I smiled, shut the astrology book and told him not to worry about going to prison as that would not happen. I apologized and said I couldn't tell him anything more than that. He left like a frightened rabbit. Tragically, I heard a short while later that he had been decapitated by a falling tree whilst driving his car.

Untapped Creativity

A talented man with a brilliant mind, who works in the scientific field, came to me for help after seeing me on a TV show. I will call him Max. He was so modest and displayed such humility which belied his incredible gifts. Sadly, for many years, his loved ones believed that he had a mental illness. He was in fact experiencing overwhelming mystical states which he found too difficult to describe in words. In such states he would sometimes succumb to panic and even cry out uncontrollably. I was able to assist him by persuading him not to dread these states but to accept them as occurrences which are natural and inevitable in our spiritual unfoldment. I discussed with him the use of prayer, breath control and meditation as an aid to applying in our daily lives, what transpires when we travel in and out of altered mental states.

He once said to me "The universe is singing and we are its song."

This incredible gentleman is an accomplished and well known physicist. Could he become one of our new scientific community currently aiming to bridge the gap between science and spirituality?

Visit By A Relative From Beyond

I know an extraordinarily talented artist, a contemporary landscape painter whom I have been friends with for many years now. We often would engage in wonderful lengthy conversations and one evening we had been sitting enjoying a glass of wine at his art studio.

As we sat chatting and eating nibbles, his grandfather in spirit came very clearly into my view. So strongly was his presence in the room that I had to tell my friend that his grandfather was around him and that just now he was speaking to me.

My artist friend listened as I went on to describe his relative who was now talking about things he had owned during my friend's childhood and memories he had shared with him as a boy. It was beautiful. I also told him that his future partner was to be a foreign lady, which indeed was what happened sometime later. On a couple of occasions, I have communicated in the dream state with my artist friend and he has told me in great detail confirming what I have shown to him, when we have next spoken.

Destined Indiscretion

Many years ago I met Debbie, a delightfully amusing and spiritual lady through a faux pas of mine at a party. I told her there and then what I had seen around her but rather indiscreetly, although I perhaps should not have done so. On reflection, my indiscretion was probably meant to be. What I had conveyed to her had been so accurate that she wished to discuss things further regarding some extremely personal issues.

There is a time and a place for everything and the intelligences controlling human destiny wanted her to know what I had revealed. I went to her house and we sat and drank tea. Most creative people have such a sense of style and she was no exception. I sat opposite her and as I was looking on and as she reclined on her sofa, another woman took over her body completely, so much so that I couldn't see the lady I was there to read for at all but only the vivid form of this woman in spirit, who quite promptly told me her name and that she was a relation to the lady before disappearing.

I was then once again staring wide eyed at the lady I was reading for still reclining on the sofa with her tea. She seemed to notice I was a bit stunned and asked if I was okay. So I told her what had just happened and she thought it hilarious and was thrilled to hear from her Great Aunt in spirit who had literally just shown up. Many messages were revealed that day and a very special friendship between the lady and me has continued ever since.

Soul Connection

This is a deeply sad story involving two brothers I will call Gareth and Karl, the elder of whom sadly took his own life after some years of drug abuse. Karl the youngest of the pair, whilst still grieving for his brother started to drink excessively. This can be a common phase when one loses a loved one, but if alcohol is then coupled with the use of hallucinogenic substances, unintended opening up to psychic influences could prove dangerous or even fatal. Hallucinogenic substances energize the user and can tear the veil to other realms. For the untrained this could prove deadly.

One night the younger brother, under the influence of drugs and alcohol, found himself in a state where he could see and hear his elder brother Gareth in spirit. The older brother called out to his sibling and recounted how much he missed him and then beckoned him to 'come over' and be with him. He encouraged him to take his own life and join him in spirit, which sadly, young Karl did.

Healing The Past

One session when I was helping a lady proved to be upsetting and embarrassing. Cheryl was married with two young sons at the time I gave her a reading. She said she wanted help on various matters but when I tuned in, a very sweet little girl in spirit with long brown hair showed herself clearly to me; and made it known that she was a lost child of Cheryl's, who had had an abortion some years before. I had to relay this information as gently as possible to Cheryl, who then became most uncomfortable and distressed. Apparently she had not revealed the abortion to anyone, not even to her husband, and it was obvious that she felt awful about her decision. Once she had calmed down, she seemed a little relieved and even grateful that this matter had come to light as a great emotional weight had now been lifted, since of course she now knew that her unborn daughter was safe and well in spirit.

Healing Case Studies

The following cases are connected with healing in one way or another. My work as a spiritual counsellor and medium has at times involved situations where I have had to apply alternative therapeutic techniques in aiding clients to achieve holistic healing.

I feel I should add that since each individual is answerable to Divine Law, illness may be prolonged as a means of assisting the person to step back from daily life to contemplate and learn some key spiritual lessons. Consequently, a medium with the gift of healing people psychically should always seek Divine guidance and sanction, otherwise one may be interfering with how a person's destiny is to manifest for their ultimate good.

Also one person might go for healing sessions regularly and enjoy and feel the benefit, but another person could go and feel no benefit at all or feel unnerved and unsettled afterwards. Some could go for one single session and be healed entirely.

The Healing Monk

This gem of a story is in relation to Gerry, a very dynamic attractive lady who had been to me for readings several times but now felt she needed a healing session due to a variety of emotional problems spilling into her private life. I was directed by spirit to apply hands on healing and after a few minutes an unfamiliar looking monk appeared in the room and motioned for me to leave.

I was flabbergasted at his appearing and telling me what to do when I had never even seen him before but stayed silent and then The Great One quickly assured me telepathically that I was to leave the room as the monk had suggested. So very quietly, I walked out, leaving the lady all by herself with the monk. After fifteen minutes or so, I was prompted to go back into the room again and gently bring the lady's focus back to the here and now.

When she opened her eyes she said, "Do you know Cher, I had the most amazing experience and saw a monk standing here healing me". I was dumbstruck and told her that I was sorry for leaving her on her own but that the monk himself had instructed me to leave the room. She was ecstatic, thrilled by the experience and felt wonderful.

The Healing Power of Love
Very recently, I gave a necklace and matching set of earrings to a friend of mine, as a birthday gift. She said that she loved them and thanked me and that was that. A few weeks later whilst she was on holiday with her young family, her little son fell and broke his leg and was screaming in agony. Intuitively she grabbed the necklace I had given to her as a gift and gave it to her little son to hold for comfort. The moment he held it in his hands, he stopped screaming and his pain stopped.

My friend was amazed and delighted and decided to wear the matching earrings to keep herself calm as they made their way to the hospital for her son's leg to be set in plaster.

She sent me a text message shortly after the event to relay the story to me and to ask me if the necklace and earrings I had given to her were magical as her son had remained calm and pain free for as long as he held it and his leg was able to be set in plaster without discomfort. I just told her that things that are given with love can be very powerful.

The healing is up to spirit, not me. If I could choose who should be healed, I surely would have healed my parents!

Parallel Realities

This remarkable series of events took place when a couple of friends went on a mountaineering trip. The man that stepped out of our 'time' was quite fanatical about physical fitness but back then, he wasn't interested in exploring the psychic and spiritual side of his nature at all. In fact he assured me that he had no idea that anything of the kind could ever happen to someone, let alone that they should happen to him. He and his friend had pitched their tent near a fairly high peak to sleep in overnight and although it was chilly, it was a calm night. He woke up first on that most memorable of mornings and decided to step out of the tent for a stretch and to take in the morning view.

When he looked out he found the scenery breathtaking. After a few minutes he realized he could see something in the distance and could even hear a sound coming from that direction. As it came clearer into view, he saw that it was a man, a very large man, in fact an absolutely huge man that was stomping steadily towards him. He thought the huge man looked nomadic and appeared to be extremely angry as he came storming upwards with what appeared to be a large weapon in his hand.

Our mountaineer started to panic and called out to his friend in the tent, but when no response came and he turned around to run back and wake him he saw that the tent and his friend had vanished!

He was now paralyzed with fear as the nomad was fast approaching and he wondered if being so petrified, he was imagining that the tent and his friend had disappeared. So he decided to go and stand on what he felt was the exact spot on which their tent should now physically be, but all the while the nomad was taking greater strides to reach him. Our mountaineer started to run around frantically on the spot yelling and calling out to his friend for help when suddenly to his relief he was back in the tent with him.

This type of experience is a classic time-shift event and is known on rare occasions to happen to healers as well as trance mediums. One of the key differences between time-shift and astral travel, is that in the time-shift the person is still in the tangible physical field of exposure. They are just in another time or era, either past, future or even parallel; whereas with astral travel, the journeys are not experienced in the dense physical field but in the invisible realms.

Openings like these are uncommon but can happen at anytime and to anyone. The key is to always have a spiritual anchor so one is prepared as much as one can be for any eventuality. The stronger our spiritual anchor, the more guidance and protection we will have. A seeker, who may not believe in the possibility of a reality switch into another realm or time frame would do well to remember that we will all one day leave this physical dimension and then experience the ultimate switch into a wider multidimensional realm.

Final Words

Each day, I tap into the energy pool that is perpetually pulling infant humanity in its upward climb towards the transcendent whence we came, and which is unceasingly nursling each and everyone of us in its bosom of boundless love. The love that surpasses egotism and all the frailties of humankind.

Unconditional Love is the acme of the Divine spark, the spirit within us. It is eternal and invisible and cannot be weighed or measured. Love is the antithesis of selfishness, jealousy, avarice, lust and deceit. All of which manifest as aspects of the human condition. It is this love that is forever kindling within us the supreme virtue of harmlessness, born out of humility, altruism, self-sacrifice, compassion and respect for the sacredness of life in its totality; to embrace not only the human but also the animal kingdom. The pinions of love are beckoning us all to rid our vision of the illusion of separateness, so that we can share in the only true joy and happiness, which alone will confer ultimate liberation from our human condition.

B O O K S

O is a symbol of the world, of oneness and unity. In different cultures it also means the "eye," symbolizing knowledge and insight. We aim to publish books that are accessible, constructive and that challenge accepted opinion, both that of academia and the "moral majority."

Our books are available in all good English language bookstores worldwide. If you don't see the book on the shelves ask the bookstore to order it for you, quoting the ISBN number and title. Alternatively you can order online (all major online retail sites carry our titles) or contact the distributor in the relevant country, listed on the copyright page.

See our website **www.o-books.net** for a full list of over 500 titles, growing by 100 a year.

And tune in to myspiritradio.com for our book review radio show, hosted by June-Elleni Laine, where you can listen to the authors discussing their books.